AN ILLUSTRATED GUIDE TO

FUTURE FIGHTERS

AND COMBAT AIRCRAFT

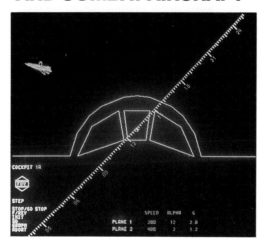

a Salamander book

Published by Arco Publishing, Inc.
NEW YORK

AN ILLUSTRATED GUIDE TO
FUTURE FIGHTERS
AND COMBAT AIRCRAFT

Bill Gunston

A Salamander Book

Published by Arco Publishing, Inc., 215 Park Avenue South, New York, N.Y. 10003, United States of America.

© 1984 by Salamander Books Ltd., 27 Old Gloucester Street, London WC1N 3AF, United Kingdom

Library of Congress Catalog Card Number: 84-71015

ISBN 0-668-06065-4

All correspondence concerning the content of this volume should be addressed to Salamander Books Ltd.

Credits

Author: Bill Gunston, former Technical Editor of *Flight International,* Assistant Compiler of *Jane's All The World's Aircraft,* contributor to many Salamander illustrated reference books.

Editor: Philip de Ste. Croix
Designer: Tony Dominy

Color two-view drawings: David Palmer © Salamander Books Ltd.
Color VSTOL engine drawings: © Rolls-Royce Ltd.

Photographs: The publishers wish to thank Headquarters, USAF Aeronautical Systems Division, Wright-Patterson Air Force Base; NASA; and all the official governmental departments, and aircraft, engine, and weapon systems' manufacturers who have supplied photographs and drawings reproduced in this book.

Typeset: The Old Mill, London
Printed: Henri Proost et Cie, Belgium

Contents

Introduction

This book is believed to be the first commercially produced hardback review of aircraft not yet built. It deals specifically with military aircraft, though some of the technologies — such as USB, upper-surface blowing, and the stopped-rotor X-wing — have obvious civil potential.

It is easy to get carried away by the technical interest and novelty of all kinds of possible future aircraft, but the title of the book is "Future Fighters and Combat Aircraft" and this is the central theme. The introductory chapters concentrate upon the technologies of the air-combat aircraft now being designed, or proposed, for the period after 1990.

One of the new options which modern technology has given the fighter designer is the ability of such aircraft to operate from any reasonably firm and level surface, or a small pad on a ship deck, or even a mechanical pivoted arm reaching out from a ship and clipping on to the top of the aircraft. Aircraft that can do this are called STOVLs (short takeoff, vertical landing), and their main advantage is that at any

Glossary

A
A/A Air-to-air
AAM Air-to-air missile
ACAP Advanced composite airframe programme
active Emitting EM radiation
ADC Air-data computer
AFTI Advanced fighter technology integration
A/G Air-to-ground
AI Airborne interception
ALCM Air-launched cruise missile
AMI Italian air force
AOA Angle of attack, angle at which wing meets oncoming air
ARBS Angle-rate bombing system
ASM Air-to-surface missile
ASPJ Advanced self-protection jammer
ASW Anti-submarine warfare
ATF Advanced Tactical Fighter
ATO Assisted takeoff
Awacs Airborne warning and control system

B
BIT(E) Built-in test (equipment)
BVR Beyond visual range
bypass ratio Turbofan ratio of bypass cold airflow to hot flow through central core of engine

C
camber Curvature of a surface in an airflow
canard A foreplane, horizontal control surface ahead of the wing
CAP Combat air patrol
CAS Close air support
CBU Cluster bomb unit
CCV Control-configured vehicle
CFRP Carbon-fibre reinforced plastics
CG Centre of gravity
CNI Communications, navigation, identification
COD Carrier on-board delivery
Comed Combined map and electronic display
Comint Communications intelligence
conformal Shaped to fit closely against aircraft exterior
CRT Cathode-ray tube
C³I Command, control, communications, intelligence/IFF
CTOL Conventional takeoff and landing
CW Continuous-wave EM radiation

D
DARPA US Defense Advanced Research Projects Agency

DBS Doppler beam sharpening
DCoS Deputy Chief of Staff
DECM Deception (or defensive) ECM
dedicated Used for that particular purpose only
DFC Direct force control
digital Calculating by numbers or other discrete bits of information which are counted, not measured
DoD US Department of Defense
dogtooth Sharp kink in leading edge of wing or tailplane to generate a strong vortex
doppler Radar making use of shift in frequency of signals reflected from Earth ahead of or behind aircraft (to give measure of true groundspeed) or of signals received from fixed (Earth) and moving targets, to give MTI

E
ECCM Electronic counter-countermeasures
ECM Electronic countermeasures
Elint Electronics intelligence
EM Electromagnetic radiation (includes radio, radar, light and heat)
EO Electro-optical
ESM Electronic support (or surveillance) measures
EW Electronic warfare

F
FAB Brazilian air force
FAC Forward air control(ler)
Fast Fuel and sensor, tactical
FBW Fly by wire, ie electrical signalling
FLIR Forward-looking IR
FOV Field of view
FR Flight refuelling
FSW Forward-swept wing
FY US financial year (ends 30 June)

G
g Acceleration due to Standard Gravity, 9.8m/s², unit of linear acceleration
GHz Gigahertz, thousands of millions of cycles per second
GP General-purpose (bomb)
GRP Glassfibre reinforced plastics

H
hardpoint Local region of structure strengthened and adapted to carry a pylon or other external load
HAS Hardened aircraft shelter, offering some protection against non-nuclear attack
HDD Head-down display, ie inside cockpit

given moment the enemy cannot be sure where they are.

Yet for political reasons such aircraft are generally (ie, in those countries influenced by the USA) regarded as "inefficient", and inferior because of small percentage penalties they suffer by comparison with CTOL (conventional takeoff and landing) fighters. So at present virtually all the studies for future fighters revolve around machines that cannot operate except from existing airbases. The argument assumes that an enemy would merely send over attack aircraft which would crater the runway(s). So the new fighters, costing tens of millions each, are being designed to "take off between the craters" on airfields targeted by anything from four to 20 missiles each.

We are not talking only about nuclear weapons. There are many things an enemy can do apart from merely making craters. In Afghanistan, for example, we have seen widespread use of a tar-like material which, when a tyre runs across it, bursts into flames. It has been used to close roads, but it is obviously equally effective in closing runways during the crucial hours that matter. FAE (fuel/air explosives) have also demonstrated overpressures that would flatten our costly HASs (hardened aircraft shelters). It is against this background that the value of the aircraft in this book must be assessed.

---

hi High altitude, typically over 30,000ft, 9km
Hotas Hands on throttle and stick
HSD Horizontal situation display
HSI Horizontal situation indicator
HUD Head-up display
Hudwas HUD weapon-aiming sight

I

IFF Identification friend or foe
ILS Instrument landing system
INS Intertial navigation system
IOC Initial operational capability
IR Infra-red, EM radiation longer than deepest red light and sensed as heat
IRCM IR countermeasures
IRWR IR warning receiver

J

jammer ECM emitter designed to smother hostile emissions

K

kHz Kilohertz, thousands of cycles per second
kT Kilotonnes yield of nuclear device
kW Kilowatts, unit of DC electric power

L

LAD Low-altitude dispenser
Lantirn Low-altitude navigation and targeting IR for (or at) night
LE Leading edge
Lerx LE root extension (hence LEX)
LGB Laser guided bomb
LL(L)TV Low light (level) TV
lo Low altitude, as low as safe to fly, typically 200 to 1,000ft, 90-300m
LRMTS Laser ranger and marked-target seeker
LST Laser spot tracker

M

MAW Mission adaptive wing
MFD Multifunction display
MHz Megahertz, millions of cycles per second
MoD(PE) British Ministry of Defence (Procurement Executive)
MRM Medium-range missile
MTI Moving-target indication, radar can eliminate returns from all except moving targets
Mux bus Multiplex digital data bus

N

NASA US National Aeronautics and Space Administration
nav/attack Used for navigation and to aim weapons against surface target

O

OKB Soviet experimental construction (ie design) bureau

P

passive Non-emitting
PCB Plenum-chamber burning
PD Pulse-doppler radar
PNVS Pilot's night vision system
pod Streamlined container for equipment carried outside aircraft
PRF Pulse-repetition frequency

R

R&D Research and development
RBC Rapid-bloom chaff
RCS Radar cross-section, apparent size of target to radar
RDT&E Research, development, test and evaluation
RHAWS Radar homing and warning system
RPV Remotely piloted vehicle
RWR Radar warning receiver

S

SAM Surface-to-air missile
SAR Search and rescue, synthetic-aperture radar
SARH Semi-active radar homing
semi-active Not itself emitting but homing on radar or other signals reflected from a target
signature Characteristic 'fingerprint' of every emitted waveform or EM signal
SLAR Sideways-looking airborne radar
smart Self-guided, especially homing on target illuminated by laser
SRM Short-range missile
stealth Technology for reducing all signatures (visual, radar, IR etc) close to zero, to make aircraft difficult to detect
STO(VL) Short takeoff (and vertical landing), hence STOL

T

taileron Tailplane (horizontal stabilizer) in left/right halves able to function as both elevators and ailerons
TFR Terrain-following radar: hence TF flight, TF mode
TRAM Target-recognition attack multisensor
2-D Two-dimensional jet nozzle with constant profile across its width
TWS Track while scan

V

VAS Visual augmentation system
VG Variable geometry, especially pivoted swing-wing
VSD Vertical situation display
V/STOL Vertical or short takeoff and landing, hence VTO(L)
VTA Soviet military air transport force

The Shape of Wings To Come

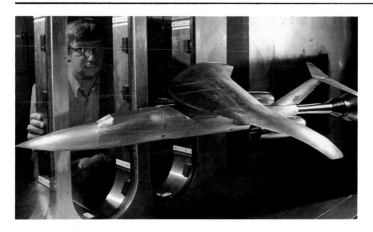

Above: A high-speed tunnel model of a proposed Mach 4·5 parasol-wing design, in which nose shockwaves are intended to be focussed favourably on the leading edge. Achieving the lift/drag benefits of such interaction is probably impossible in combat manoeuvres.

GENERALS and aircraft designers prefer to solve the simpler problems, and shelve the difficult ones. At present, while fighter speeds are no higher than in the mid-1950s, we are presented with new possibilities opened up by dramatically improved engines, radical new structures, and wholly new avionics which knit together the entire aircraft, its systems and its weapons in a way that appears at times to make the pilot superfluous. So the future is bright and exciting; yet in other ways, we have no idea where we are going.

Today few observers of the scene would insist that the pilot really is becoming superfluous, yet almost 30 years ago this was fast becoming the official view in Britain, which in April 1957 final-

Below: Studying the aerodynamics of a Mirage 2000 during the drop away from the wing pylon of a Matra Magic close-range AAM. Such testing, in this case at France's ONERA national research centre, has to be carried out for each type of store expected to be carried.

ly announced that fighters were henceforth obsolete, and would no longer be built. In their place the RAF would use missiles.

Today we appear to know better (though the British aircraft industry never fully recovered from that disastrous period), and design teams all over the world are busy with exciting new fighters which show how strong are the dictates of fashion. The need, it appears, is for an aircraft that, instead of destroying its enemies at a distance of many miles, has to close to "eyeball" range and zoom round the sky trying to outfly its enemies like the Red Baron, using a gun and close-range missiles. Close range means violent manoeuvre, and violent manoeuvre means low speed, typically in the region of 350 knots (400mph, 645km/h). Probably the best dogfighter would be a biplane, but nobody has the nerve to propose one. In any case it would be nice to fly at over Mach 2 in order to race quickly towards the enemy — which is thought a sensible thing to do — and modern combat aircraft are so expensive that they have to fly more than just the one mission. The obvious alternative

mission for a fighter is some form of ground attack, and this calls for quite different avionics and sensors, the highest possible speed and either a tiny wing or, better still, no wing at all, (ie, one that retracts), reliance being placed on body lift to apply the necessary vertical accelerations to keep the speeding aircraft just clear of the ground.

Yet the dogfighter needs an enormous wing in order to pull more g than the enemy at all heights, which is the exact opposite of the attack aircraft, and it also needs a high-mounted pilot with the best possible all-round view, and many other features which are quite different from those of the low-level attacker. Of course, there may be no reason for anyone to climb into the stratosphere in future, because this is where SAMs can (so most people think) unfailingly knock out any aeroplane foolish enough to go there. Even the SR-71 "Blackbird" at over 2,000mph (3220km/h) at 80,000ft (24400m) would pose no special problem to hundreds of Soviet SAM batteries, unless the USAF carries countermeasures cleverer than anything we know.

Below: A tunnel model of the McDonnell Douglas Model 279-3, which could be the next generation STOVL (short takeoff, vertical landing) combat aircraft after the Harrier II. Much research will be needed to perfect vectored-thrust induced flow round the canard and wing.

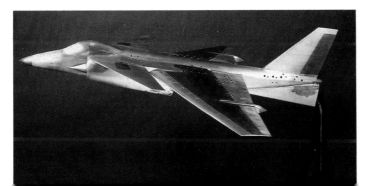

In fact a hint that perhaps this speed and height no longer offers much protection is provided by the USAF's renewed interest in what used to be called "aerospace planes" and now have the more impressive title of TAV, transatmospheric vehicles. It is generally believed in the USAF that, because the timescales between consecutive weapon systems are being forced by inflation to get longer and longer, the ATF (Advanced Tactical Fighter) may be the last "fighter" for that service to be designed to remain always within the atmosphere. Obviously, flight beyond the atmosphere into space will complicate fighter design further, at the very least by demanding attitude-control rockets and possibly a complete space propulsion system with throttle modulation so that the pilot can choose when, where and how he returns to Earth.

For the moment, ATF alone offers problems enough. It does not need great imagination or resources to draw impressive future fighters; schoolboys do it in the backs of their exercise books. One feels there is a trace of the enthusiastic schoolboy

about many of the ATF proposals. They typically would weigh 150,000lb (68 tonnes), be over 100ft (30m) long and not only have extremely poor agility but would cost billions to buy and maintain. At the other end of the scale a persevering team in Switzerland earnestly believes air forces will soon be forced by simple considerations of cost to turn to smaller, simpler fighters, and they have for years been trying to sell their little Piranha — so far without success.

Though it would be nonsense to suggest there is a kind of ATF-versus-Piranha battle going on in the minds of fighter designers, it is certainly true that the wealth of possibilities open to us make decisions difficult to take. A very few of the new possibilities seem certain to be used to the full.

1 Basically unstable (or RSS, relaxed static stability) design, using an instant-reacting flight control system to keep the aircraft under control and pointing the way it is travelling.

2 Some form of thrust vectoring in the engine nozzle(s), used both in flight and for augmented steering and braking after landing (see page 29).

Below: The ACT (active controls technology) Jaguar now flying at Warton is the most advanced unstable aeroplane in the world at present, with a degree of longitudinal instability never previously dared. Trying to fly it has been likened to sitting on the bonnet of a high-speed car while pushing a reversed bicycle by the handlebars!

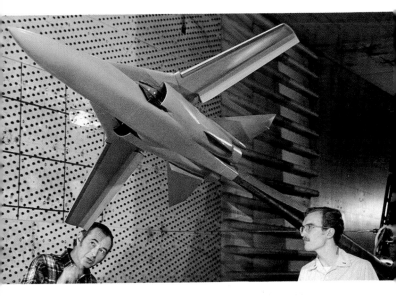

Above: Taken at Arnold Engineering Development Center, this shows a model of the Boeing MAW (mission-adaptive wing) now fitted to a rebuilt F-111A.

Below: Yet another BMAC research project is this F-16 carbon-fibre front end for studies into how best to protect advanced avionics systems against lightning strikes.

3 Some form of variable geometry (ability to change shape), for example by having a wing with variable camber (which is in fashion) or variable sweep (which is out of fashion).

4 Flight controls with a geometry which can move the aircraft bodily up/down or left/right without altering the attitude of the fuselage (so-called DFC, direct force control).

5 Advanced avionics for continuous precision solutions to the problems of navigation, air-to-air

gunnery, air-to-surface weapon delivery and how best to avoid hostile defence networks.

6 Advanced composite materials which offer not only better ratio of strength and stiffness to mass but which also can be tailored so that, under flight loads, the structure bends and twists in the most favourable way.

7 Low-drag weapon carriage, as discussed in the section on Sensors and Weapons (see F-15 picture on pages 34-5).

8 The ability to fly the aircraft without any limits up to AOA (angle of attack) well beyond the normal stall without the slightest worry over loss of control, incipient spin or overstressing the structure.

9 A modern cockpit, almost devoid of traditional instruments, which puts the pilot in the ideal posture for air-combat manoeuvring and tells him everything he wishes to know and nothing else.

10 All technologies and techniques, both in the conceptual design stage and in hardware, that reduce cost and the need for any maintenance or attention, while increasing reliability.

Obviously, most of these desirable objectives could be built into an ATF looking rather like a military version of Concorde, and alternatively into a more affordable Piranha. One can perhaps equate the two extremes financially by the relationship "One ATF = 50 Piranhas". Those with long memories will recall the emergence of the Folland Gnat 30 years ago. This tiny fighter showed performance and agility fully equal to any of the big competition, and better than most, for ludicrously small costs and maintenance effort. Yet the RAF and British officialdom scorned it absolutely, adducing many totally irrelevant arguments to support the contention that a small or cheap fighter must be inferior. In fact the only country to use the Gnat in war, India, found it an excellent air-combat fighter with a better ratio of kills to losses than its immediate rival back in the early 1950s, the Hunter!

In the same way, any ATF project engineer would regard the Harrier and Sea Harrier as relics of a bygone age, almost unbelievably crude in their robust simplicity. Yet, as the Soviets know, this is what wins wars. Had a few billion dollars-worth of ATFs been in the South Atlantic in 1982 they might have found it difficult to operate without

Below: A typical preliminary study for an ATF, this Grumman Aerospace sketch shows a moderate-Mach supercruise fighter with the almost mandatory canards and rear 2-D vectoring nozzles. The inlet would be good from all aspects except the vital one of stealth.

AWACS support, difficult to recover back on a small deck or front-line airstrip with 200ft (60m) visibility, and difficult to keep flying round the clock with maintenance done in the teeth of a blizzard. Admittedly, the way that conflict opened, with a stick of "iron bombs" dropped blind across a runway, is unlikely ever to happen again. Those who cling to the idea of "taking off between the craters" are in for some nasty surprises.

But what about the shape of our fighter? Assuming it is a CTOL we still have to choose whether we are going for BVR (beyond visual range) kill capability or for dogfight agility. The fashion today is the latter, and this virtually dictates the whole design; but the USAF lays stress on the ability to cover large distances at high speeds in the bracket Mach 1·5 to 2·5. It is this demand, called "supersonic persistence", that seems likely to result in fighters that are big, heavy and incredibly costly,

Below: Swiss artwork showing a twin-engined Piranha heading out over the Alps. The private group promoting this small fighter have so far failed to persuade any customer that their philosophy is correct.

Flight-control elements

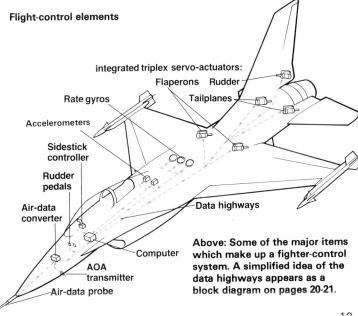

Integrated triplex servo-actuators:
Flaperons   Rudder
Tailplanes

Rate gyros

Accelerometers

Sidestick controller

Rudder pedals

Air-data converter

Computer

AOA transmitter

Air-data probe

Data highways

Above: Some of the major items which make up a fighter-control system. A simplified idea of the data highways appears as a block diagram on pages 20-21.

because of their fuel capacity. Going back to 1959 the USAF insisted on a 3,300 nautical mile ferry range for its supposedly agile world-beating TFX, leading to an F-111 so heavy and cumbersome it ceased to be a fighter at all. Clearly the expensive lesson has not quite been learned. It is better to build a small agile fighter with a good ratio of thrust to weight; then, if absolutely necessary, it can later be made to carry very heavy loads. The F-15, for example, weighs 41,000lb (18600kg) as an interceptor but 82,000lb (37200kg) as a bomber!

An accompanying sketch shows the variety of shapes that can appear on the designer's rough pad when he is starting out on a new study. We cannot even take it for granted there will be a fuselage, because "stealth" aircraft tend to be all-wing. If there is a wing it can be of roughly normal chord or it can extend almost from nose to tail, as in the F-16XL. It may be preceded by a Lerx, and there may be a canard ahead of it; this is almost certain in a modern CCV design with artificial pitch stability, and the use of a canard in conjunction with wing trailing-edge movables (called flaperons, elevons or possibly separate flaps and/or ailerons) at one stroke gives enhanced agility, reduced structural stress, less trim drag, better control at extreme AOA and, not least, DFC to change the trajectory instantly in any direction, or maintain the trajectory and change the direction in which the fuselage is pointing. This capability may be enhanced by having a separate horizontal tail.

Today the fashionable shape is a fighter with a clearly defined fuselage housing two engines, with inlets on top if it is a stealth design and on the sides or underneath if it is not, with a canard used as a primary control surface close-coupled (ie not far removed longitudinally) to a main wing tapered on the leading edge and with variable camber. The wing profile will certainly be of the modern supercritical form, which reduces weight, leaves more room inside for fuel and dramatically reduces drag as soon as shockwaves start to form (which occurs later than on a conventional "peaky" wing). A supercritical wing on a fighter is almost forced to have variable

Below: Though the money involved is not large, by the standards of modern programmes the unique shape of the Grumman X-29 makes the element of technical risk relatively high. To fly before this book appears, this small research aircraft could just prove the key to a completely new family of fighters better than any predecessor.

camber, both the leading and trailing edges being hinged. The MAW (mission-adaptive wing), being tested on an F-111, does its best to approach the ideal of a truly flexible wing with a smoothly curved lower and upper surface, instead of having a rigid central section and sharp discontinuities at the hinges to the front and rear panels.

One aircraft in this book, the X-29, is testing the FSW (for-ward-swept wing). If it performs "for real" as it does in tunnel models, Grumman hope it will give them a significant advantage in the design of future fighters, though it would be premature to say it has made other fighter wings obsolete. In theory it offers less drag at all speeds than ordinary wings, as well as better manoeuvrability, shorter field length and many other advantages including mak-

Below: Today's fighter designer has a wealth of possible choices, such as: A, nose strake; B, Lerx; C, conventional nozzle; D, 2-D vectoring nozzle; E, fixed canard; F, moving canard; G, flapped canard; H, tailplane/elevator; I, slab tailplane; J, taileron (stabilator): K, variable-camber wing; L, droop/elevon delta; M, cranked arrow wing with slat, flap and aileron or flaperon; N, VG (variable-gemoetry) wing with glove vane, slat, low-speed flap and roll-control spoiler; and O, stealth design with flat underside and no separate fuselage.

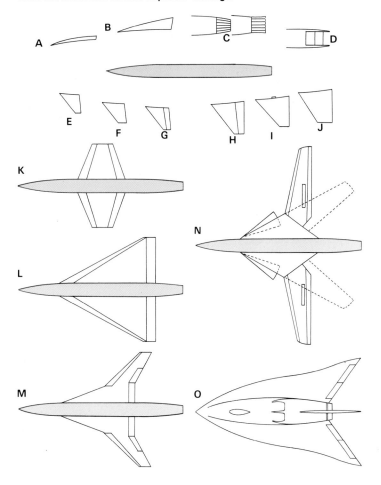

Above: Computers are needed to draw the optimum arrangement of cutout parts from carbon-fibre composite sheets. This machine working on Harrier II parts at McDonnell Aircraft cuts four to six layers at a time, and stores 50 programs, each lasting up to two hours.

ing the aircraft essentially spin-proof. The reason why the FSW is so unusual is that until recently it has been impossible to realize: as soon as an FSW aircraft pulled g in a turn the wings would bend upwards until they tore off because, unlike other wings, the AOA increases as the wing bends. Today it is possible to build composite wings using skins of graphite (carbon) fibre and other directionally aligned materials, to tailor the "grain" of the wing plies so that deflection of the wing under load does not cause catastrophic increase in AOA and resulting "divergence" which would tear the wing off.

There are powerful and potentially highly beneficial effects possible in the favourable interaction of propulsive jets and the flow round the wing, and these are discussed in the chapter on Propulsion. In theory such interaction, by multiplying the lifting power of a wing, could enable a fighter to use a smaller wing and still meet its required turn radii for air-combat. Such an aircraft would be much better in the low-level attack mission, because as explained earlier the attack aircraft needs the smallest

possible wing area, and especially the smallest span.

In the 1960s it was agreed that the VG (variable geometry) swing-wing was the perfect answer, in that the long-span outstretched wings that are efficient in subsonic cruise or low-speed tight manoeuvres could be folded back to give an ideal dart-like shape for the Mach 1 dash at treetop height. Today this has gone out of fashion, mainly because policymakers that once saw the benefits now see only the modest penalty in structure weight. A possible alternative is the so-called pivot or scissor wing, which in current studies for low-altitude penetrators can fold flush into the top of the fuselage. This has obvious benefits for stealth reasons in that the radar signature is minimised. An alternative that fits in better with the dogfight scenario is the CCV canard with totally artificial stability and DFC. The canard and DFC wing flaps can work together to take out most, if not all, of the frightening and potentially destructive buffet caused by high-speed flight through dense turbulent air. It may not eliminate the high-frequency

Above: The original full-scale mock-up of the BAe Agile Combat Aircraft (which had twin fins). The wing is likely to have a major contribution by Aeritalia who want to get experience of carbon-fibre composites. What Europe really needs is a viable programme.

Below: One of the best ways to design a low-level bomber is to give it a slew wing, pivoted at the centre. In the supersonic attack mode the wing is retracted into the top of the fuselage, which itself provides all the lift. Stealth qualities would be outstandingly good.

buzz, but it takes out the real whoppers that are the ones that — quite apart from considerations of pilot comfort — destroy weapon-delivery accuracy and eat into airframe fatigue life.

It is possible to be absolutely dogmatic and state that fighters that are described as also flying the attack mission — such as the F/A-18A Hornet and Mirage 2000N — are at best severe compromises. They are incapable of flying such missions at transonic speed at treetop height. Later in the decade they may grow extra systems for taking out the vertical accelerations in the way that the B-1B is designed to do (and that has a VG wing, anyway). At present a fighter with a big wing and no active DFC system to take out the bumps simply cannot fly the low attack mission except at partial throttle and in great discomfort.

Cockpits

Right: The cockpit of
the GD/USAF
AFTI/F-16 is not very
different at first glance
from that of an F-16C.
But compared with an
F-16A the changes are
major and include: two
MPDs (multi-purpose
displays), a wide field
HUD, helmet-mounted
sight and associated
electronics, voice-
interactive electronics,
and added switches
on the Hotas throttle
and sidestick
controller.

THROUGHOUT history combat aircraft have got more and more complicated, and by the mid-1950s they had also been made so fast that (except for specialized high-flying reconnaissance platforms) the peak dash speed has stayed the same ever since. For more than 20 years the steady improvement in hostile defences has forced attack aircraft to fly as low as possible, yet today even the lowest-flying aircraft can be shot down by fighters from a higher level. Thus, no matter whether we consider the defence missions or the attack missions, the number of decisions to be taken per unit time have tended to increase, often sharply, while there has been an inevitable movement away from the "Red Baron" style of flying (totally "seat of the pants" judgement and application of human skill, born of experience) to the modern style in which almost everything rests upon streams of pulses of electricity we call digital bits.

Today the main debate about fighter crew workload centres around how many humans are needed. There is one outstanding example — the F/A-18A Hornet — of an aircraft planned from the start to fly multiple missions with one man, and it attempts to do this by having a very modern cockpit. Bearing in mind that electronics is not exactly a new art, and that combat aircraft with CRT (cathode-ray tube) displays and many other advanced features were operating in World War II, it is remarkable how poor by comparison are many of the front-line aircraft in use today. They still confront the pilot with rows of clock-dial instruments which each have to be studied and interpreted in order to discover if they are indicating something important. Control levers and knobs are scattered all over the place, with no uniformity (except for stick and throttle) between different aircraft types, and often arranged to facilitate grabbing the wrong control in an emergency. Pilots have to remember large numbers of vital actions or numerical values, usually stored in their head. Not least, after

Left: One of the tools for the study of future fighter cockpit displays is the Magic at USAF Aeronautical Systems Division (Flight Dynamics Lab). Magic stands for microcomputer applications of graphics and interactive communications. Sharp-eyed readers will recognise the external stores display to the right of the pilot as being that reproduced at lower left on page 23. Magic cranks in the latest ideas as they are invented.

making an attack run through intense hostile fire, they would then find that no ordnance had in fact departed because their own input, or the interface switchology, had malfunctioned. (Even if bombs did release correctly, official analysis after the hostilities revealed that in the Falklands war some 36 per cent failed to detonate.)

Since 1960 a few visionaries have seen the way to improve matters, and since about 1975 the modern fighter cockpit has gradually matured. Its position in the aircaft tends to be dictated by aerodynamic shape, the common (but not inescapable) practice of placing the main radar ahead of it and the fuselage fuel behind, and the need for the best all-round view without imposing enhanced vertical or lateral accelerations in air-combat manoeuvres. Modern multilayer polycarbonate canopies almost big enough to cover a family car are light in weight yet can restore their original shape after a Mach 1 impact with a "standard bird".

Inside the cockpit the pilot reclines in a backward-sloping ejection seat with his feet on pedals at the same level, an attitude giving good resistance to hard and sustained vertical accelerations which in the latest fighters can reach 9g. The idea of enclosing the crew in ejectable capsules is no longer in fashion, though the contemporary seat may later be replaced by a separable aircraft nose with its own microprocessor and flick-out control/drag surfaces. This might be lighter, and would save the pilot's life in the low-level inverted position.

As he reclines in his comfortable seat the fighter pilot in the en route phase of his mission is relaxed and does not have a severe workload, yet he is still required to study various visual inputs, take numerous decisions and often translate these into physical control actions commanding the systems, weapons, propulsion or aircraft trajectory. In future he will become more of a passive overseer, a mission manager, just as he was (in theory at least) in the F-106 interceptor designed prior to 1956. To change his status needs im-

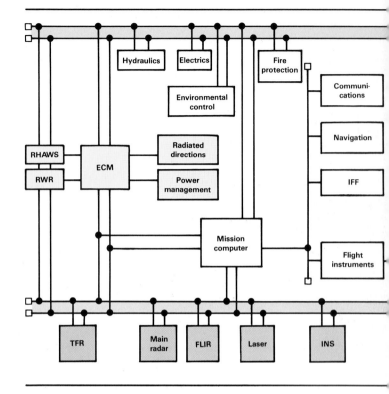

proved avionics and displays.

Traditionally all functioning items in the aircraft are connected not only by their own electric power cables, hydraulic or other fluid pipelines or other power links such as hot-air ducts, but also by individual control wires handling small electric data or control currents. More than 25 years ago it was clear that a better arrangement was necessary, and the first major change was to introduce the concept of the serial data bus. This is one or more coaxial cables along which pass streams of various kinds of information, coming from sensors, or the aircraft systems or even the pilot. The flow is multiplexed, in that for a few thousandths of a second the information flow comes from source A; an automatic switch then feeds information from source B; then it samples C, followed by D, and so on. Suppose we wish to know

the amount of fuel in a tank; in the old days a wire from the tank contents gauge was continuously linked to an instrument in the cockpit, but with a multiplexed data bus the information is sampled in brief instants separated by perhaps one second of time. In today's cockpit the pilot can call up the information and get it at once, relayed by the same bus that, in between whiles, also carries hundreds of other measured values or other data.

The diagram shows a typical "Mux Bus" arrangement in greatly simplified form. The actual architecture would be vastly more complicated. Moreover the whole idea has now had to undergo a second revolution to keep pace with today's VHSIC (very high-speed integrated circuit) avionics and VLSI (very large-scale integration) microprocessors which in tiny packages are now handling 1,000 times more information

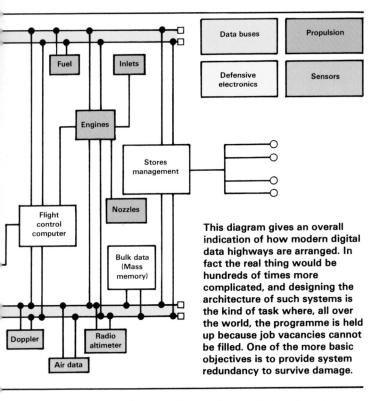

Data buses

Propulsion

Defensive electronics

Sensors

Fuel

Inlets

Engines

Stores management

Nozzles

Flight control computer

Bulk data (Mass memory)

Doppler

Radio altimeter

Air data

This diagram gives an overall indication of how modern digital data highways are arranged. In fact the real thing would be hundreds of times more complicated, and designing the architecture of such systems is the kind of task where, all over the world, the programme is held up because job vacancies cannot be filled. One of the more basic objectives is to provide system redundancy to survive damage.

than in complete fighters 20 years ago.

For a start coaxial cables have been replaced by bundles of thousands of fibre optic "light pipes". Use of light multiplies the rate at which data can be transmitted, and the typical loom an inch or so (25mm) in diameter can transmit data many millions of times faster than a coaxial cable. It becomes possible to build in duplication to take care of damaged data paths, and to keep data flows intact even after severe battle damage. The need for fibre optics did not arise from such data as fuel tank contents but because of the growth in capability of main radars, EW/ECM systems and similar major data sources, together with a multiplicity of amazingly fast computers, which at a conservative estimate mean that the rate at which data passes round the 1990s fighter will be 20 million times today's rate.

The rapid data flow does not stop in the cockpit but links all parts of the aircraft, usually in both directions. For example, whereas in a fighter of today the pilot's stick and pedals are connected to push/pull rods or cables, new fighters now being built have FBW (fly by wire) control in which the input commands are transmitted as small electrical signals along fine wires (typically duplicated and physically separated flat ribbons). We expect the 1990s fighter to have FBL (fly by light) control in which the commands are transmitted by fine optical fibres. Such near-instantaneous transmission is vital in future fighters because they will be of basically unstable design which would swap ends and disintegrate if there were to be any delay in the continuous flow of control commands.

No pilot could hope to fly such an aircraft manually. Actually

Above: A tandem two-seat cockpit being used by Boeing Military Airplane Co to refine the design of cockpits for future tactical combat aircraft. Wide-angle HUDs and various computer-generated HDDs (head-down displays) may be combined with helmet displays.

producing a totally unstable fighter is a design and engineering task of the first magnitude, but the payoffs are enormous. When British Aerospace converted a Jaguar to FBW in October 1981 the pilot, Chris Yeo, said "Response was instantaneous, and despite quite strong turbulence remarkably smooth". A year later Yeo was investigating "carefree manoeuvring" of the kind most fighter pilots would envy, knowing that he could never induce a flick, stall departure or spin even with asymmetric external stores at impossible AOA and with the harshest control inputs. Now he is well into the final exploration with previously unprecedented instability of −10 to −12 per cent, with 0·25 ton ballast in the tail and giant leading-edge strakes. In this form the Jaguar might have been thought unflyable, but Yeo's initial assessment was "We have marked improvement in performance, especially at takeoff and landing. There is less drag, and a significant improvement in the turn rate".

It is obvious, as some people have known all along, that all except the simplest aircraft should be built this way. Once active controls are fully proven and accepted we shall see unstable airliners which will save passengers having to pay for millions of gallons of fuel a year which at present are burned in overcoming unnecessary kinds of drag. What is not so obvious is whether the F-16 is the first fighter to have the new standard sidestick controller on the side coaming of the cockpit, with a comfortable rest for the pilot's arm and, if he chooses, also his wrist, or whether it is an oddball that nobody will copy. At present for example, BAe at Warton are firm in adhering to the traditional central stick, though this may well be of the force-sensing type which commands the aircraft according to the force applied by the pilot, without actually moving visibly.

Certainly one technique where there is no argument is HOTAS (hands on throttle and stick). This simply means that every control that the pilot might need to use during air combat, and possibly during the entire mission (though this is less certain), is not scattered just anywhere around the cockpit but is found in the form of a button, lever, trigger, knurled rotary switch, rolling ball or other kind of input already close under his fingers and thumbs on either the throttle(s) or on top of the stick. Thus, with a little practice, he can pole the aircraft round the sky without having once to look inside the cockpit to find an urgently needed control input. Everything is already literally at his fingertips, and he can work it without looking and almost without conscious thought, in the same way that a car driver requires no conscious thought (we hope) to find the brake pedal.

As for the displays facing the pilot, these have lately undergone a revolution. For over 60 years the main "progress" in cockpits was to add more and more instruments, the only difference between them being that while most had circular dials some had linear tapes. The possibility of perhaps replacing some by one or more larger screens giving a pictorial display was investigated in World War II by the RAE at Farnborough, and just after the war by Wright Field, but it seemed rather "far out" and the necessary technology was only beginning to emerge. Today the F/A-18A is in service with an almost completely pictorial cockpit, and developments for the immediate

future are a matter of degree.

Accompanying pictures of displays by BMAC (Boeing Military Airplane Co) show a stage slightly later than the F/A-18A. The VSD (vertical situation display) is seen in an attack mode, the aircraft in white being shown the way to go by a white flight profile ahead leading to a cleft in the hills. Green terrain is below the flight level and brown above, while hostile emitters show yellow, the regions of greatest threat being red. Another display format shows the stores situation. ECM pods and tanks are shown, along with two AAMs and four unselected bombs. Eight bombs which have been selected come up yellow, and nose or tail fuzing shows green (here they are fuzed at both ends). The next stores to be dropped are marked by small triangles. Should one hang-up it will immediately turn red.

Anything else you'd like to know? The pilot has only to ask, because it is now accepted (at least by the USAF and Dassault-Breguet) that the fastest way of interfacing with one's aircraft is by human speech. Much work is being devoted to interpreting both the sense and the urgency of spoken commands, including sudden vague expletives, and also in synthesizing correctly spoken responses.

Below: A suggested IMPD (interactive multipurpose display) showing the external stores carried and the status or condition of each. Some of the basic features of this display are outlined in column 2 of the text.

Below: Also described in the text above, this BMAC VSD (vertical situation display) is hoped to lead to the idealized presentation of information to guide an attack pilot through defended hostile airspace at the lowest safe level.

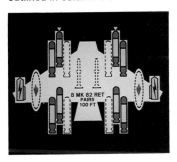

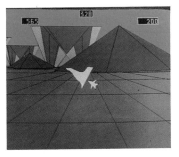

Propulsion

Above: Demo 1A is one of the Turbo-Union RB199 advanced growth engines; this research could lead to the next generation XG40 engine, proposed for EFA.

Below: A control-room monitor at the USAF Arnold Engineering Development Center providing a view of afterburner combustion in simulated supersonic flight.

CONTINUED progress in gas-turbine technology is reflected in each new generation of fighter engines being smaller, lighter, simpler and more reliable than their predecessors. Not much can be done about diameter and frontal area, so the main visual change in fighter engines over the past 25 years has been reduction in length. Two engines which are strictly comparable in power are the General Electric J79 and Turbo-Union RB199, both rated with afterburner at about 17,000lb (7711kg) thrust. The J79, used in the F-4 and F-104, has a diameter of about 39in (991mm) and length of 208in (5·3m); the new RB199, used in the Tornado, is 34in (870mm) in diameter and only 127in (3·23m) in length. The J79 has a ratio of thrust to weight of about 4·4, while the RB199 ratio is up to 8·6.

The next generation of engines will be even more compact, have fewer parts, yet provide similar power by handling greater airflow and running at even higher turbine gas temperatures, using single-crystal blades held in powder-metallurgy discs and using advanced techniques for cooling and for maintaining the absolute minimum clearance between the fixed and moving parts through which air or gas under pressure would leak. Of course all modern engines are of modular design, assembled from several easily separated major sections so that, should a fault develop, the offending module — which may be compact and light enough to be manhandled — can be replaced without changing the whole engine, and in many cases while leaving the rest of the engine in the aircraft.

Ports are provided for borescopes so that the interior may be inspected visually with the engine installed, and health monitoring systems instantly give warning of any irregular condition or impending failure, before it happens. Usually any urgent news is flashed to the pilot, with recommended action to take; other information, with the fullest diagnostic analysis, is stored for readout by maintenance personnel.

Another feature of all new fighter engines is completely digital electronic control. Electronic engine control is not new, and was a feature of the Britannia of 1952, but like the whole field of microelectronics we are on the brink of a revolution using fairly recent technology. The future fighter engine will have a control system similar to the aircraft itself, with multiple redundancy to survive failures and total integration to link not only all parts of the engine but also link them with the rest of the aircraft (see simplified data bus diagram on p.20). Modern digital engine controls improve engine efficiency, smoothness of operation and safety, and reduce fuel consumption. They extend engine life and significantly enhance aircraft performance, especially following any kind of failure in the propulsion system. As in future fighters, they also enable the engine to operate in ways that are unstable, or at least impossible to control by previous manual/hydromechanical methods, which at last enable the propulsion system to realise its full potential.

Below: Almost hidden amongst special testbed equipment is the Turbo-Union RB199 Demo 1A engine, at right, blasting in full augmentation (reheat) into a tunnel cooled by water sprays. A remote-control camera took the picture to record the flame.

Above: The first prototype of the SNECMA M88, which with mainly M53-type accessories made its first run in January 1984. This two-spool augmented turbofan is intended to power the next-generation fighter from Dassault-Breguet to follow today's Mirage 2000.

Engines themselves have always got smaller and lighter for a given thrust, the most dramatic improvements being in the combustion section. Modern engines have a heat-release rate per unit volume of combustion chamber more than 1,500 times that in the first Whittle turbojet (which itself was far beyond anything in previous technology in this regard). Many of today's fighters, especially in the Soviet Union, still use turbojets. Bypassing air from the low-pressure compressor, or fan, past the rest of the engine to rejoin the hot core flow in the afterburner has the advantage of giving better fuel economy at low subsonic Mach numbers which account for about 98 to 99 per cent of the total flight time. Fuel economy, and also power, are improved in such conditions by increasing the engine pressure ratio. In older fighters pressure ratio seldom exceeded 10, but in today's engines it varies up to 24 for the RB199 and F100 despite the competitive thrust/weight ratio for these engines of 7·8 and 8·6 respectively.

France has always laid stress on the propulsion needed for over Mach 2, which calls for a slim engine with bypass ratio of far below unity and a low pressure ratio. Such engines are quite uncompetitive in terms of overall mission fuel, and they have also tended to be heavy. When the F-16 was being designed the big F100 engine was chosen mainly because of its use in the F-15, but it was found that its fairly high bypass ratio of 0·7 also enabled the F-16 to fly much further than any rivals such as the YF-17 or F-4. Future engines will certainly stick to bypass ratios of around 0·7, as well as high pressure ratios of at least 25, but by using advanced blade design with a wide chord it is possible to achieve high pressure with fewer stages of blading. This simplifies the engine, reduces costs and makes it tougher and better able to withstand combat damage.

One important trend is to increase dry (non-afterburning) thrust. Though modern afterburners can increase thrust by anything up to 100 per cent (in the case of the RB199) they burn tremendous amounts of fuel and send out a giant flame astern through the wide-open propulsive nozzle. Tomorrow's fighter is going to find the sky much more perilous than today, and it will survive only by the most complete adherence to stealth principles, and these are concerned not just with radar signature but with all emissions including IR. The radiation from an engine in full afterburner makes life really easy for enemies, and there are strong grounds for believing that afterburners will become part of history.

We can thus begin to form an idea of the basic fighter engine of the 1990s. Similar in diameter to current engines, it will be very much shorter and lighter, remarkably simpler (with perhaps three fan stages and four or five compressor stages) yet still working at a pressure ratio greater than 20, with a mass of new materials and technologies and totally integrated by microprocessors. The bigger ones will have a thrust of about 25,000lb (11340kg) without using an afterburner, but they may still have some form of variable geometry, the most likely place being the core nozzle which discharges the hot gas from the core surrounded by the cooler bypass air. In the past this nozzle has been fixed, the bigger nozzle downstream being variable to cater for use of afterburner. Now

Above: Outdoor testing at Shoeburyness — a remote Ministry firing range on the Essex coast — where the noisy PCB Pegasus is making up for lost time. Here the PCB front nozzles are being angled downwards. Often such testing is done with the engine inverted.

Below: Today the PCB Pegasus is installed in a gantry-mounted Harrier airframe for research into air and gas flows and reingestion at different heights and attitudes. Water sprays are used to cool the concrete slab on which the hot gas jets impinge.

Above: A Pratt & Whitney mock-up model of a future fighter engine with a 2-D vectoring nozzle. This company has done extensive running with such nozzles and, with rival General Electric, has a 50-month $202,750,000 development contract.

the positions may be reversed, the main nozzle being fixed but the core nozzle being variable, to adjust not only the core but also the bypass duct. The microprocessors will keep altering this nozzle for peak efficiency and minimum fuel burn.

Though the main nozzle may in future, with no afterburner, be of fixed area, it is in fact likely to be of a totally new type able to vector the jet around a wide arc. Vectored thrust was pioneered by the Pegasus engine, which apart from the engine of the Yak-36MP (Forger) is unique in being able to lift the aircraft off or return it to the ground as well as drive it at transonic speed. The USAF has consistently ignored

this vital capability, but in about 1976 it suddenly noticed one of Whittle's ideas from about 1940: the possibility of vectoring the single nozzle of an otherwise conventional engine to control the trajectory of the aircraft. In its modern form this kind of vectored nozzle moves only in the vertical plane. The first actual hardware was built by Rolls-Royce and MTU in about 1966, using such engines as the RB153. Today's nozzles differ in being of 2-D (two-dimensional) form, rectangular instead of circular so that the upper and lower parts can be made in the form of hinged flaps. Inevitably this box-like nozzle is heavier than the structurally better circular type,

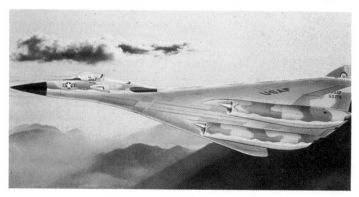

but it enables the entire jet to be pointed anywhere from about 20° up to 20° down, and with further effort it is possible to achieve at least double these deflections.

A deflected jet imparts an extremely powerful attitude control force as well as contributing to propulsion, independently of the airspeed. One regime where the deflected jet is of great value is takeoff. Believe it or not, the typical fighter of the 1970-85 time period accelerates on takeoff to the speed at which wing lift will overcome the weight at a speed at which the tailplanes still cannot rotate it to the nose-up takeoff attitude! A 1990 canard will do better, but with a deflected jet it is possible to rotate the aircraft to takeoff AOA at exactly the right airspeed, thus greatly reducing takeoff run. (Of course, flying manually a pilot would risk misjudging it and stalling the aircraft back on the ground, but with tomorrow's automated data-bus everything happens precisely according to the book). Jet deflection in combat can prove very beneficial at extremely low airspeeds, for example in stall turns and similar manoeuvres, while on landing a 2-D nozzle is easy to equip with a reverser which can be used in the approach regime. Coming in with the throttle at high power and in full reverse gives the shortest ground roll possible, but the installation has to give reverse thrust without undesirable pitching moments. All major engine companies have conducted 2-D vectoring nozzle tests, and today no self-respecting US artist would dream of drawing an ATF (see entry later in book) with old-fashioned circular nozzles!

Left: An artist's impression of a Rockwell ATF with twin vector-nozzle engines. The inlets are bad from the viewpoint of radar reflectivity, but excellent for performance at high AOA.

Right: A 2-D vectoring nozzle. In the drawing at right the nozzle is deflecting the jet upward, while in the upper drawing the jet is deflected downward. If left and right nozzles of a twin-engine fighter were deflected in opposition the aircraft would roll.

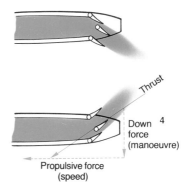

Thrust

Down force
(manoeuvre)

4

Propulsive force
(speed)

Sensors and Weapons

ELECTROMAGNETIC (EM) radiation is by far the most important medium for conveying information. Like humans, fighters can pick any of a wide spread of EM wavelengths: heat (IR), optical (light) and various radio waveforms. Each has its own advantages and disadvantages, and nobody today appears to agree with the British government's 1957 belief that such sensors could do the job without those of a human being added. In fact, most fighter pilots would say that the most important sensors are those of the pilot!

Physically usually the biggest sensor is the main radar. Thanks to developments in electronics this is getting ever-smaller, and in relation to the rest of the aircraft cheaper. Today's fighter radars tend to be modular, aircooled, highly reliable (200 hours operation in combat missions between failures) and to have upwards of 20 different operating modes. These modes fit the set for all forms of navigation, air-to-air and air-to-ground missions and the use of all the weapons nor-

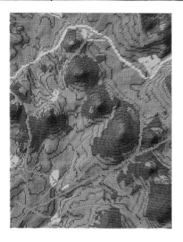

Above: This digital terrain map was developed by the US Army and is part of a joint Army/USAF test programme which includes flight testing in the AFTI/F-16. The detail and colouring are still in process of refinement.

Below: Today's fighters armed with radar-guided AAMs, such as the F-4, have to keep flying towards the enemy in order to guide the missile. Future fighters might aim radar rearwards.

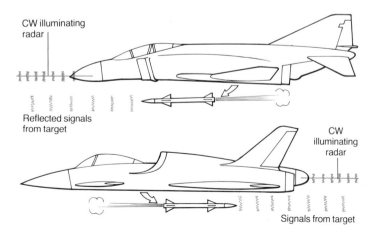

CW illuminating radar

Reflected signals from target

CW illuminating radar

Signals from target

Above: When it reaches the squadrons in late 1985 the Hughes AIM-120A (Amraam) will combine great lethality from BVR (beyond visual range) with self-contained "fire-and-forget" guidance.

mally carried, and in virtually all future fighters the radar will have the ability to lock on to low-flying aircraft seen from above and also pick one target from a dense mass (in the presence of intense hostile jamming and other interference) at BVR (beyond visual range). If possible, the maximum range against large aircraft will exceed 100 miles (161km).

Inevitably today's radars on major all-weather aircraft are intimately associated with AAMs (air-to-air missiles), because the one guides the other. Close-range dogfight AAMs can home on the IR emissions from enemy jetpipes and other areas, but so-called MRMs (medium-range missiles) home on to the fighter's own coded radar signals reflected from the enemy aircraft. A little thought will show that, with a radar mounted in the fighter's nose, this means that the fighter must fly towards the enemy all the time its own MRMs are in the air. Clearly this is a very grave disadvantage, because it throws away the possible advantage of being the first to detect the enemy, the first to achieve radar lock and the first to fire an AAM, and may result in the enemy getting off a deadly close-range AAM at the last moment.

There has been much study of ways of eliminating this need to keep flying towards the enemy. By far the best answer is to be armed with an AAM that does not need the fighter's own radar. One guidance method that confers this "fire and forget" quality is IR homing, as used for almost 30 years. Another is to fit a small radar into the nose of the AAM. The only Western active-radar AAM at present (and for almost 20 years past) is the AIM-54 Phoenix, but this is matched only with the F-14 Tomcat and is a very costly weapon. Now at last the effectiveness of many Western fighters will be multiplied by arming them with AIM-120A Amraam (advanced medium-range AAM).

This is obviously going to be the No 1 AAM in most Western air forces over the next two decades. A direct replacement for AIM-7 Sparrow, it is in fact appreciably smaller, being shorter and of 7in (178mm) diameter instead of 8in (203mm), the weight being about 326lb (148kg) instead of over 500lb (227kg). Thus, it will be easier to carry in multiple, and the really important thing is that it will bring stand-off kill capability to fighters not fitted with large target-illuminating radars. AIM-120A flies towards its target on a simple strapdown INS (inertial navigation system) until, near its chosen target, it switches on its own small radar and homes by itself. By this time the fighter that launched it might be almost 100 miles (161km) away, heading for home.

Of course, as with all fire-and-forget weapons, AIM-120A must be matched with absolutely unambiguous target-identification and IFF (identification friend or foe) equipment. Many fighters operate under close control from ground stations or from Awacs type aircraft which can pass complete information on the location and character of other aircraft within about a 230mile (370km) radius. Those that have to operate autonomously, without such help, need sensors able to furnish positive identification of aircraft type and character. Thanks to the unequalled power and range of their AWG-9 radar fire-control the Grumman F-14A was the first aircraft regularly fitted with a VAS (visual augmentation system), called the Northrop TVSU (TV sighting unit). It gives

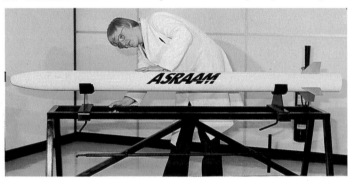

Above: Short-range partner to Amraam, Asraam, seen here as a full-scale mock-up, is being developed as a standard NATO AAM, including use by and production in the USA, by a team led by BAe (UK) and BGT (Germany). There are no forward control fins.

Below: The BAe Dynamics Alarm (advanced lightweight anti-radar missile) is not only potentially more lethal and versatile but also much smaller than rival weapons. This round is hung on a Tornado, which can carry four in addition to a full bomb load.

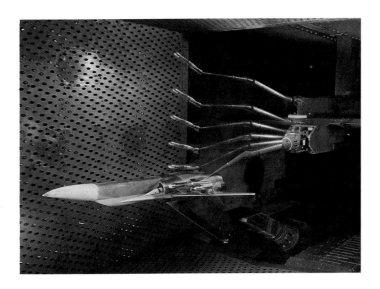

Above: Studying the separation of a store — apparently an AGM-109 cruise missile — from an inverted F-111 model in a high-speed tunnel. At the correct windspeed an arm moves under computer control to simulate the missile's departure behaviour.

a magnified image in the cockpit of other aircraft even at night or in bad weather, typical fighters being identifiable as to aircraft type at a range of some 15 miles (24km), at which they would not be detectable to the human eye unless they were high up leaving a vapour trail. Just how the future VAS will work appears to be classified; it may use any of a number of EM wavebands.

If killing at a distance is the obviously preferable objective of all combat aircraft, the ability to win in a close dogfight is still regarded as essential to most air forces, even though this is a perilous situation where (quite apart from the quality of the aircraft or pilot) it is extremely difficult in a real war situation to be sure of doing much better than trade aircraft roughly one-for-one. (Both the Falklands and Bekaa Valley campaigns were quite different from what might happen in Central Europe.) Here the AAM for the future, in the West at least, is likely to be Asraam (advanced short-range AAM), being developed by a UK/German team, with US participation and

with France as a formal observer. Again, this is to be a compact all-aspect fire-and-forget missile, with low pilot workload and the ability to be carried in clusters. It can be fired at large off-boresight angles, and its unique guidance and control enables it to make violent manoeuvres from the moment it is fired. Many older AAMs, though they could pull far more g than any aircraft, could in fact be outmanoeuvred because of the great difference in flight speed (provided the fighter pilot had ice-cool nerve and accurate information on AAM relative position). Asraam will never be outmanoeuvred by any target aircraft.

Though for most purposes very high supersonic speed is not only difficult to attain, and extremely costly in fuel, but also positively undesirable, there is a general measure of agreement that many future fighters will need to be able to cruise for long distances at supersonic speed — typically around 1·8 — in order to get within firing parameters with their weapons. In this particular phase of flight, aircraft drag is extremely important, because the acceleration and speed reached depend on the probably small difference between propulsive thrust and aircraft drag, and reducing the latter by, say, 10 per cent, may make a difference of 100 per cent in the margin of excess thrust. Thus there are great pressures to do away with AAMs and other stores hung on wing pylons, where drag is high. Instead the F-15 even today has FAST packs which carry extra fuel in conformal (shaped flush against the fuselage) pallets, with AAMs snug against the lower body chines. The old F-4 showed how large Sparrow AAMs could be recessed into the underside of the fuselage, while of course it is always possible to design the aircraft with an internal weapon bay. The RAF's Tornado F.2 follows the F-4 recessed AAM formula, but ATF solutions have yet to emerge. Certainly it will no longer be good enough just to stick Sidewinders on the wingtips and Sparrows on pylons.

Continuing improvement in the power and discrimination of radars has already led to the situation in which hostile aircraft can be detected and positively identified at ranges too great for the fighter's weapons. This is the case even where MRMs are carried, typical range for Sparrow and Sky Flash being around 25 miles (40km). By the 1990s there will be an urgent need for active-homing AAMs with an auto-

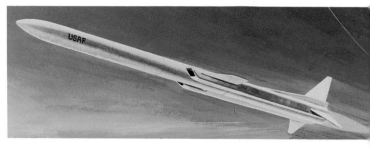

Above: Artwork by the CSD (Chemical Systems Division) of United Technologies shows the appearance of a typical vehicle in the DRED (ducted rocket engine development) project. This is one of many in the USA, France and West Germany all aimed at replacing rockets by air-breathing ram rockets of various kinds. The airflow mixes with a fuel-rich gas produced by the solid rocket fuel to yield a high-energy jet with much greater efficiency than a plain rocket.

Right: The future F-15E DRF (dual role fighter) will be cleared to fly at 81,000lb (36740kg). This picture of a development aircraft shows the low-drag "conformal carriage" of bombs or other stores along the lower edges of the body, which also carries FAST packs which add over 9,000lb (4082kg) of fuel.

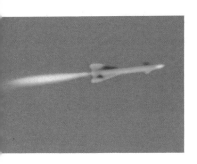

Left: Teledyne Ryan's Firebolt flies at high altitudes at Mach numbers up to 4 on the sustained thrust of a CSD hybrid propulsion system using both nitric acid and a solid fuel grain. Vehicles of this kind can fly faster and further than those with normal rocket propulsion, and the propellants will not burn on contact without external-source ignition.

nomous range of at least 100 miles (161km). With rocket propulsion the weapon comes out very large and heavy, Phoenix being in the 1,000lb (454kg) class. As the AAM flies all its mission in the atmosphere it is only common sense to use air-breathing propulsion, which dramatically extends the range for any given size of AAM. It has the further big advantage of keeping the propulsion operative throughout the flight, so even at extreme range the speed and manoeuvrability are if anything better than at the start, whereas with today's AAMs the motor burns out, the missile coasts, the speed falls away and soon it cannot turn as well as its target.

Typical future long-range AAMs will use air-breathing propulsion. Some such weapons are being designed to use ramjets; an alternative is the CSD DRED (ducted-rocket engine development). This is fired as a solid-fuel rocket, accelerating rapidly away from the launch aircraft. The fuel produces an over-rich gas which is then diluted by fresh air rammed in through the inlet. This then burns as a very efficient ramjet, giving full-thrust propulsion which can be throttled over a thrust range from 18 to 1, giving flexible propulsion for all conceivable future AAM missions, and with thrust duration typically six to eight times as long as for today's rocket motors.

Aeritalia/Aermacchi/ EMBRAER AMX

Origin: Joint programme by Aeritalia Combat Aircraft Group and Aermacchi SpA of Italy, and EMBRAER of Brazil.
Type: Tactical attack and reconnaissance aircraft.
Engine: One 11,030lb (5003kg) Rolls-Royce Spey 807 turbofan produced in Italy under licence by Fiat, Piaggio and Alfa Romeo.
Dimensions: Span (over AAMs), 32ft 9·75in (10·0m); length 44ft 6·5in (13·575m); height 15ft 0·25in (4·576m); wing area 226sq ft (21·0m²).
Weights: Empty 13,228lb (6000kg); max loaded 25,353lb (11500kg).
Performance: Max speed with full external mission load at sea level 723mph (1163km/h. Mach 0·95); cruising speed in bracket Mach 0·75 to 0·8; takeoff run at max weight 3,120ft (950m); attack radius with 5min combat and 10 per cent reserves with 6,000 (2722kg) of external ordnance (hi-lo-hi) 320 miles (570km), (lo-lo-lo) 230 miles (370km).
Armament: Total external load of 7,716lb (3500kg) carried on centreline pylon, four underwing pylons and AAM wingtip rails; internal gun(s) (Italy) one 20mm M61A-1 with 350 rounds, (Brazil) two 30mm DEFA 5·54 with 125 rounds each.
History: Start of design studies 1977, start of bilateral development January 1981, first flight (Italy) 15 May 1984, (Brazil) 1985.
Users: Brazil and Italy.

An outstanding design, with considerable export potential, AMX's chief missions will be surface attack in support of friendly ground and naval forces, and reconnaissance, but it also promises to have considerable capability in long-range interdiction and self-defence air combat roles. It is subsonic, but so are almost all aircraft when flying a low-level attack mission with a heavy external weapon load. By not attempting to exceed Mach 1 in the rather unusual high-

Below: Two-view of AMX in the Brazilian configuration, with two 30mm guns. Stores pylons are fitted but empty, though Sidewinder AAMs are shown in place on the wingtip rails used only for these close-range weapons.

Above: Six AMX prototypes are being built, Nos 4 and 6 being assembled in Brazil. No 1 flew on time but was damaged beyond repair in a forced landing on 1 June 1984. The second was to fly in September 1984, the programme staying on schedule.

level clean mission, the AMX comes out vastly smaller, cheaper and more efficient, and certainly with better field performance and greater agility. It was originally designed by Aeritalia and Aermacchi in Italy to partner the Tornado and F-104S, but in late 1979 Brazil realised it followed exactly their own thinking and EMBRAER came in as 30 per cent partner, based on the FAB's requirement for 79 aircraft compared with the AMI's need for 187. The work-split is broadly: Aeritalia (46 per cent), centre fuselage, fin/rudder, elevators, flaps, ailerons, spoilers and radome; Aermacchi (24 per cent), forward fuselage and rear fuselage; and EMBRAER (30 per cent), wings, slats, tailplane and inlets. The Rolls-Royce fan engine is fully qualified and in production by an international consortium based mainly in Italy.

When one compares the AMX with aircraft which it will replace, such as the G91, A-4 Skyhawk and Hunter, the effect of modern technology becomes impressive. AMX is remarkably small, even in comparison with its much less capable predecessors, yet it combines very much greater mission radius with a heavier and more varied load of ordnance. The wings are particularly small, for minimum drag and gust response at full power at low level. Yet by the use of large double-slotted flaps which run out aft of the wing on tracks, in a way slightly resembling the Fowler flap, the AMX promises to be able to use bomb-damaged runways and front-line airstrips, even with full weapon load.

The entire aircraft is modular, as is the engine, and different customers can modify particular parts so long as the interfaces are kept intact. The AMI has chosen a Litton INS, while the FAB prefers to stick to traditional VOR navigation (despite the fact that INS would be far more useful in the vast undeveloped inner regions of Brazil).

Particular care is going into the avionic systems carried for weapon delivery, EW and reconnaissance. The nose is occupied by a small ranging radar produced by FIAR in Italy on the basis of an Israeli Elta set, the EL/M 2021 pulse-doppler set used in the Kfir. For reconnaissance, provision is made for three interchangeable pallets (either panoramic, photogrammetric or TV) to be quickly installed in a special bay in the forward fuselage, while IR and optical sensors can be carried in a pod on the centreline pylon. The Italian AMX will have very complete Litton/OMI/Selenia stores management and weapon-aiming systems, and an Elettronica active and passive EW installation.

The first AMX, assembled in Italy, flew on 15 May 1984. Six prototypes are being built, Nos 4 and 6 being assembled in Brazil. Full combat service in both countries should be achieved in 1988.

ALR Piranha

Origin: Arbeitsgruppe für Luft- und Raumfahrt, Switzerland.
Type: Light fighter.
Engine: See text; data for RB199 Mk 104 augmented turbofan of 16,000lb (7257kg) thrust.
Dimensions: Span about 24ft (7·3m); length 37ft 9in (11·5m); height 14ft (4·25m); wing area (main surface) 240 sq ft (22m²).
Weights: Loaded (air superiority mission) 15,190lb (6890kg).
Performance: Max speed (clean or AAMs only, hi) 1,320mph (2124km/h, Mach 2); takeoff run (air superiority mission, SL) 1,150ft (350m); landing run (with drag chute) 1,250ft (380m); initial climb 59,000ft (18000m/s); typical combat radius (attack weapons, lo-lo-lo) 280 miles (450km).
Armament: One internal gun (30mm Oerlikon KCA preferred); seven external stations for 4,410lb (2000kg) of weapons, including AAMs and all normal attack weapons.
History: Study in progress since 1975.
User: Not yet funded.

A competent and largely professional group in Switzerland has devoted much time and private money to promoting an attractive lightweight fighter in the belief that there is a large (3,000-4,000 units) global market for such aircraft. Many of the advantages of a small fighter are obvious: lower costs of acquisition and ownership, lower training costs, higher serviceability, reduced vulnerability in combat and probably enhanced agility, and many others.

At first the Piranha was as small and simple as possible, and an early propulsion choice was two Larzac M74-07 augmented turbofans. This gave way to the RT.172-58 Adour, and pressure of increased mission demands and higher performance has now forced concentration on the RB199 with the GE F404 as a second choice. Inevitably this puts the Piranha squarely into the same class as the superficially similar JAS39. How, then, can this private proposal hope to succeed?

ALR would reply that their project is even smaller and simpler than the Swedish aircraft, and also offers significant advantages over the F-20A Tigershark and other existing aircraft. It has a flapped canard and wing trailing-edge "flaperons" all controlled by a digital FBW system, though the dogtooth wing leading edge is fixed. By 1984 the wing had grown in size from the 16m² of all previous studies to the figure given above, to achieve higher sustained and instantaneous turn rates. If ever an unofficial fighter project deserved to succeed, this does, if only for the decade of effort behind it.

Below: Ground-to-air photographs of free-flight model tests of the current configuration of Piranha. In the modern world it is doubtful that any private group could do more to promote a fighter aircraft proposal than ALR have done.

Above: Model of the so-called Piranha 6, powered by a single RB199. This was the first close-coupled canard agile fighter proposal to be drawn up, the configuration being dated 1978.

Below: High-speed tunnel model ready for testing at Zurich.

Antonov An-400 (Condor)

Origin: OKB of O.K. Antonov, Soviet Union.
Type: Ultra-heavy airlift transport.
Engines: Four 51,650lb (23430kg) Lotarev D-18T turbofans.
Dimensions: (estimated) Span 243ft 6in (74·2m); length (without prototype nose-probe) 236ft 3in (72m); height 65ft 7in (20m); wing area 7,800 sq ft (725m²).
Weights: (estimated) empty 397,000lb (180080kg); max 882,000lb (400075kg).
Performance: (estimated) Cruising speed 497mph (800km/h); range with max payload 4,970 miles (8000km).
Armament: None.
History: First flight, probably late 1982; entry to service 1985.
User: Soviet Union.

In recent years the one obvious gap in the Soviet Union's spectrum of aero engines has been a large HBPR (high bypass-ratio) turbofan, which in turn has held back the development of the largest transport aircraft. In the mid-1970s it was clear such an engine would be available from the Lotarev team, and the Antonov OKB (experimental construction bureau) accordingly went ahead with a giant new cargo aircraft.

Called "Condor" by NATO, the An-400 (an inexplicable designation) is closely similar to the USAF C-5 Galaxy in form and capability, thought it is physically larger and has more powerful engines. It is safe to assume that the vast interior has a full-section rear ramp door, but it would be unwise to take it for granted that the nose hinges up, as in the Galaxy, to provide unrestricted access at both ends. Such access would be highly desirable, and an alternative answer would be to make the nose in the form of left/right clamshell doors. Previous Soviet airlift transports have had glazed noses with seats for a navigator and/or observer, even when various radars are fitted.

Below: Official drawing by a US DoD artist showing deployment from an An-400 of SS-20 triple-warhead missiles on their mobile transporters. Condor could move such weapons rapidly over long distances.

Unquestionably the An-400 will have a multiwheel landing gear to spread the weight over the largest possible ground area. Ability to operate from unpaved surfaces has been taken for granted in almost all Soviet military aircraft, except for long-range interceptors of the Voyska PVO (air-defence force). It would be reasonable to assume that the An-400 will have even more landing wheels than the 28 of the Galaxy. Previous VTA strategic aircraft are equipped to inflate or deflate the tyres in flight according to the gross weight and the surface upon which the next landing will be made.

There has been uncertainty over the type of engines used. The 1984 edition of the DoD publication *Soviet Military Power* sticks to the assertion that ''four 44,000lb thrust Kuznetsov turbofans'' are fitted, but no such engine is known. The D-18T appears the obvious engine, and its thrust ties in well with the US-reported gross weight. What is rather less obvious is how the gross weight and payload, both higher than for the Galaxy, tally with the fuselage which is estimated to be appreciably shorter.

The first An-400 is a civil aircraft, and probably the production machines will be shared between the VTA and Aeroflot. It has been assumed that one of the chief duties of the An-400 is rapid deployment of major weapon systems over long distances, the obvious initial candidate for such airlift being the complete SS-20 long-range nuclear missile system on its mobile launch vehicle. It is said that 200 troops with full equipment could be carried (so could 500), and a third alternative would be two main battle tanks.

Below: Drawn especially for this book, this side view and plan are as accurate as possible on the very limited information available in mid-1984. Note the multi-wheel landing gears, low horizontal tail, rear gun turret and (one of the items known for certain) full-length engine fan ducts. Details of nose and rear cargo doors are unknown; the artist here has reasonably assumed an upward-hingeing nose door.

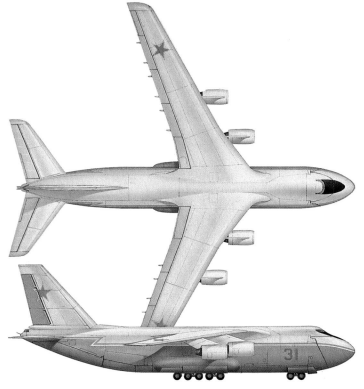

Advanced Tactical Fighter

Origin: Current (1984) contracts held by Boeing, General Dynamics, Grumman, Lockheed, McDonnell Douglas, Northrop and Rockwell.
Type: Multirole fighter.
Engines: See text for this and other aspects.
History: In 1984 seven companies were working on study contracts, each for just under $1 million, leading to a decision in 1986-87, first flight in 1988-89 and operational capability "in the 1990s".

The ATF is by far the biggest future air-combat fighter programme at present known to be planned outside the Soviet Union. It is intended to keep the USAF ahead of the competition through into the 21st century, though how this can be done becomes increasingly uncertain. The best one can strive for is to get the seven top fighter design teams in the USA — not including Fairchild Republic, incidentally — to compete with one another in the hope that a potential reward of some $50 billion will result in some really impressive proposals.

So far the outward show of the ATF programme has revolved around concepts readily understood by the media, such as the "supercruise" technique, unstable design, digital FBW (fly-by-wire) and such new shapes as the canard and FSW (forward-swept wing). Probably more important are the aspects dealing with costs and manpower requirements. The USAF has been deeply troubled by the problems of keeping its major combat aircraft ready to fly. We have been this way before, in the mid-1950s when the Century-series fighters promised performance at the cost of great complexity and financial burdens which, by previous standards, seemed astronomic. Nobody then achieved much success with smaller or simpler fighters, the one type that tried to follow this path — the F-104 — being the least successful. Today, while artists draw fighters that look like single-seat Concordes, the USAF is faced with greater problems than ever before in actually keeping readily available hardware on the flightline, and it has cast covetous eyes on such troublefree items as the US Army's T700 helicopter engine and the RAF and RN's Harrier and Sea

Below: Text describing this proposal (pre-ATF) by BMAC appears as item A on p.44. This artwork was prepared just before it became universally fashionable in the USA to illustrate new fighters with vectoring rear nozzles.

Harrier which, in the most atrocious environment imaginable, stay ready for battle with hardly any attention.

ATF is not just another programme. Even the FX (which became the F-15) was a natural response to the MiG-25, which indicated a new level of high flight performance among Soviet aircraft which in 1965 the USAF could not match, but there was no cause for significant alarm. Today the situation is very different. The emergence in service of the Su-27, MiG-29 and MiG-31 have at a stroke roughly levelled the air combat capability between the USAF and the Soviet Union, on a one-for-one basis. The USAF has the massive advantage of a head start, with over 800 F-15s and (counting NATO allies) some 1,000 F-16s, but against this must be set the Soviet output of 1,260 fighters a year in comparison with just over 300 for the USA (for all services combined). There is thus an urgent need for a new fighter to try once more to redress the numerical inferiority by technical superiority, but this time there is the extremely disturbing and novel situation that nobody knows if technical superiority is possible. ATF has to contend not with the Su-27, MiG-29 and MiG-31 but with whatever improved versions or successors will be in service in the 1990s when the chosen ATF becomes fully combat-ready. Nobody knows if the ATF will turn out to be better than the competition.

In some areas, perhaps most notably in advanced air-breathing engines, composite structures and (possibly) avionics and cockpits, the USAF probably has a distinct edge at present. In guns, AAMs, the entire spectrum of EW systems and certainly in simple and robust hardware design the advantage appears to lie with the competition. Perhaps most worrying of all, the basic design parameters must be absolutely right from the start, and the final article must be affordable in adequate numbers. Most observers in the USAF and US industry consider ATF the most important single programme for a military aeroplane there has ever been in the USA.

It would be possible to preface the following five company ATF reviews by a very lengthy preamble, because possibly more has been written on ATF than on any other aircraft that did not yet exist or even come within several years of existing. Instead the temptation has been resisted, and the reader is referred instead to the introductory chapters of the book itself.   ▶

Below: This particularly strange BMAC proposal is item B on the next page. The sharp chine, arched wings and engine nacelles interact to give a mix of area rule and compression lift (the brochure says). Engine nacelle shockwaves are focussed on the wing leading edge.

It must be emphasized that the following is based not on what five of the seven finalist companies are actually proposing in the ATF programme, which at present is classified, but on what they have seen fit to publish. Obviously some of the proposals that follow are created with an eye on projecting a forward-looking company image; it would be a disaster for the West if they were actually to be built!

BMAC

Boeing Military Airplane Company is based at Wichita, Kansas, but its Advanced Airplane Branch is located near the main Boeing headquarters in Seattle. Here various teams have done extensive work on new fighters for several years (and we should not forget that in 1923-35 Boeing was one of the world's top fighter companies). Conceivably none of the following is directly related to the BMAC submission(s) in the ATF programme, but the designs do represent serious company thinking.

A This ground-attack fighter is an AFTI (advanced fighter technology integration) scheme, with a ventral nose fin for direct lateral translation without the need for roll. In view of the small overall size the engines look remarkably slim. Outboard of them are conventional wings, which might be pivoted for roll-control; inboard is a long-chord wing carrying elevators.

B This strike fighter attempts to achieve enhanced supersonic lift/drag ratio by increasing the compression lift under the arched wings. The latter grow out of a sharp chine around the broad nose. This could also be a superior reconnaissance aircraft.

C This was BMAC's submission in a NASA study for SST technology applied to a future "European" fighter with 500 mile radius. Note the powered canard ahead of a fixed delta wing, podded engines with inlets shielded by the wing at high AOA and whose nacelles then blend into the wing and terminate in 2D vectoring nozzles, and palletized recessed weapons.

D This was Boeing's proposal in the same NASA study, but in this case for a "Middle East" fighter with a radius of 1,500 miles (2414km). This aircraft would be larger and heavier, with a cranked-arrow wing carrying pure podded engines. There is no canard, and the twin vertical tails are wing-mounted. What looks like a large weapon bay may also house the main landing gears.

E This is an even larger and longer-ranged fighter, possibly 90ft (27·4m) long and weighing about 100,000lb (45 tonnes), and thus needing engines in the 40,000lb (18 tonne) thrust class. Like the preceding machine it is tailored to supersonic

Below: This canard delta is described under entry C above. The canard, which is a primary control surface, is rather higher than the wing, which has full-span leading-edge flaps and aileron/flaps divided into front and rear portions.

cruise, and has a nose chine leading to a cranked-arrow wing with blended-pod engines. Vertical tails might be pivoted slabs. High in stealth technology, such an aircraft might serve as a stand-off killer with long-range AAMs, but it is difficult to see how it could survive in a classic dogfight unless it can play entirely new tricks.

F Totally unlike previous BMAC projects, this fighter is "optimized for low-level superiority". It has pivoted swing-wings with fully variable camber when spread for slow takeoff and landing, with roll control assisted by differential vectoring of the nozzles of the engines, which are fed by upper-surface inlets which leave the belly free for conformal weapons.

▶

Above: Described as item D on the facing page, this BMAC proposal is configured for large internal fuel capacity and peak propulsive efficiency. Landing gear might comprise bicycle main units plus stabilizer wheels under the pods.

Below: Item E on these pages, this big and extremely fast fighter has engines close under the wing, inlets thus being shielded against flow distortion at high AOA. BMAC developed this concept during studies carried out for the USAF and NASA.

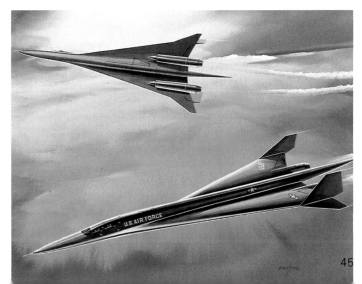

Below: Featured as item G on the opposite page, this modest-sized tactical multirole fighter is an attempt to match the FSW with 2-D vectoring nozzles and a good arrangement of stores and sensors. Mach limit would be in the region of 1·5.

Grumman Aerospace Corporation

Long famous for its naval aircraft, Grumman is going flat out to be a leader in land-based fighters, and has issued a profusion of ATF style suggestions. The company is in a unique position because of its X-29 FSW aircraft, described separately.

G This agile fighter and attack aircraft combines the FSW with two engines provided with a 2D rectangular vectoring nozzle system. The top of the nozzle forms the hinged wing trailing edge between the swept-forward vertical tails.

H A larger ATF in the supercruise class, this machine has an FSW and forward-swept vertical tails mated with a sweptback canard and 2D vectoring nozzles. The fins extend far below the wing level as in the original (unbuilt) configuration of the F-15. They might even house the main landing gears, avoiding the disturbance of the gears passing immediately in front of the engine inlets.

I This ATF dates from 1978, and is for a large fighter optimised for high-Mach supercruise (say, Mach 2·5). The very slim rear fuselage is flattened to blend into the quite high-aspect-ratio sweptback wing. There was at this time a great ▶

Left: This "all-singing, all-dancing" swing-winger is BMAC's proposal described as entry F on p.45. Unquestionably its configuration is influenced by the need for stealth low-signature characteristics, and it is much better in this regard than most of the suggestions on these pages.

Below: Perhaps the Grumman artist who drew this FSW fighter (item H in the text above) was more interested in aesthetic appeal than in avoiding excessive aeroelastic structural deflections, but if it holds together it would be most agile.

vogue for engine pods that blended into the wing and ended aft of the trailing edge with vectoring nozzles. Oddly, the canards look if anything slightly below the level of the wing.

J Having estabished a workable body with semicircular centrebody inlets leading straight through to engines mounted parallel with vectoring nozzles, Grumman mated it with every kind of wing/canard group that could be imagined. FSWs and pivoted swing-wings looked good, but this particular combination has a fixed sweptback wing and close-coupled canards. The latter are mounted remarkably low.

K A distant relative is this tunnel model designed for minimum zero-lift drag at ▶

Below: Another rather beautiful and very slender Grumman fighter, this proposal is item I. The winglet-equipped vehicle leaving a sooty trail is apparently a cruise missile launched by this "supercruise" fighter.

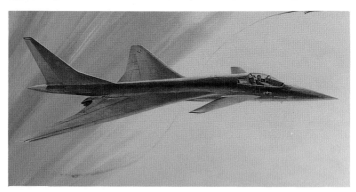

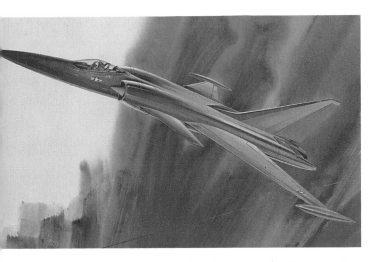

Above: This Grumman ATF-style project is discussed in the text under letter J opposite. The tip-mounted pods, and the overall shape, remind one of fighters of the early 1950s, but this is a serious conception which the manufacturer is prepared to justify.

Below: Grumman describe this tunnel model as being "developed to explore low zero-lift drag at supersonic speeds". A point not made in the text K is that zero-lift drag is considered merely for simplicity. The engines are equipped with 2-D-vectoring nozzles.

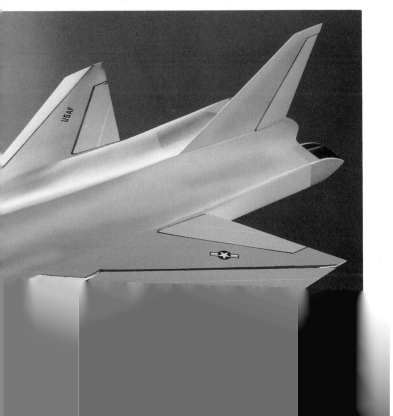

Above: As explained in the text (L, below) this Grumman design has scarfed inlets arranged to rotate through 180°; here they are in the conventional forward-slope position as in the F-14. The 2-D nozzles are shaped to minimise lower-quadrant IR signature.

▶ supersonic speeds. Large powered canards precede the F-14 type inlets leading to vectoring nozzles, and high-mounted swept wings with exceptionally large and powerful variable-camber leading flaps and trailing flaps of unusual geometry.

L This FSW fighter is one of a family fitted with engine inlets which rotate 180°. In the position shown they resemble circular versions of the F-14 inlet, with good efficiency at high AOA, as in a dogfight. Rotated 180° the inlet slopes in the reverse direction, adequate for supersonic cruise and giving minimum radar signature. The 2D engine nozzles likewise have no IR signature from below. This particular configuration has aft elevators beside the nozzles as well as canards.

M STOL takeoff by an ATF with flapped canards and backswept wings carrying vectoring engine pods. Compared with the well-proven Harrier the technology of vectored nozzles at the rear is in its infancy, and may not be practical at all.

Lockheed-California Company

This famous company has a separate entry later dealing with some of its numerous new ideas. Where ATF is concerned its outlook has certainly not revolved around total cost of ownership and maintenance manpower, but has adopted the view that the sky is literally the limit.

N Probably the biggest, heaviest and most costly fighter ever suggested, this machine could also fly reconnaissance missions. Planned to cruise at Mach 5 (3,350mph, 5390km/h) at 100,000ft (30km), its Inconel (high-nickel alloy normally used for turbojet turbine blades) leading edges glow red-hot purely from kinetic heating. Power comes from four turboramjets burning liquid methane (essentially the same as LNG, liquefied natural gas). At takeoff the engines are turbojets, but at speeds well beyond Mach 1 large valves and doors ▶

Above: This artwork showing the ATF with flapped canards (M) was supplied by Wright-Patterson AFB, home of Air Force Systems Command which not only manages ATF but is the repository of more future-fighters technology than anywhere else on Earth.

Below: Lockheed has always liked impressive ideas, and this fighter (item N in the text) is not only a monster but at full speed can heat its leading edges to over 538°C (1,000°F). The methane-burning engines are variable-cycle turboramjets.

▶ change the airflow to bypass the original "engines" and duct the highly compressed air straight to the afterburners, operating as ramjets. In the 300,000lb (136 tonne) class, such an aircraft might cost $200 million each. Whether much slower SAMs could shoot them down is still uncertain.

O This proposal, dating from 1982, is also methane fuelled. Slightly smaller, and without a separate horizontal tail, it bears close aerodynamic kinship with the SR-71 Blackbird, though it has a single vertical tail. The same flattened and blended wing/body shape is seen, and the two engines have rectangular vectoring nozzles. The airframe would be mainly aluminium alloy, much cheaper than the SR-71's titanium, though the latter would be needed for the hottest portions such as the nacelles and leading edges. The underside view shows large airbrakes under the flat forebody, but there is no indication of how weapons might be carried. Lockheed claim this ATF could fly not only interception but also deep strike missions, despite its poor Stealth quality (mainly because of the engine inlets). But with internal weapons and fuel it might be able to fly at highly supersonic speed at low level, provided its structure was strong enough and that the terrain was fairly level.'

McDonnell Douglas

Unquestionably the leading fighter house in the Western World, McDonnell Aircraft at St Louis has produced the F-4, F-15, F-18 and Harrier II. For many years the company has produced designs for supersonic and hypersonic fighters; recent ideas are featured here.

P Dating from 1977, this was one of a family of STOL fighter studies during the rather exciting period when the use of 2D vectoring nozzles was new. Of course, no such machine can have the STOVL capability and flexible basing possible with a true vectored-thrust engine, but the vertically swivelling nozzle does enable takeoff run to be reduced (in conjunction with powerful canards to lift the nose) and can have a major influence on combat manoeuvrability. This F-15 ▶

Below: This particularly fine Lockheed artwork shows Aircraft O. Most of the skin would be aluminium alloys of a new type giving improved strength at high temperatures, titanium being restricted to a few very hot places. Lockheed has "no immediate plans to develop such a fighter".

▶ size machine has the inner wings extended aft to carry the elevators. The author doubts that vectored nozzles so far from the centreline are practical; the nozzles might be reliable, but loss of an engine would mean immediate ejection.

Q Representative of the 1981-82 ATF studies at St Louis, this proposal is one of a large family with a box-like fuselage carrying high-mounted canards and tapered (but unswept) rear wing. The body sides are flat and vertical downstream of the variable lateral wedge inlets, and the engines would have 2D vectoring nozzles. A single gun is installed above the left inlet duct.

Rockwell International

Rockwell's North American Aircraft Operations is today's name for the team that produced the Mustang, Sabre and F-100. They were the losing finalists in the 1969 fight to build the F-15, and the aircraft depicted here is the modern successor to the company's entry in that programme. More than any other shown in these pages, it is a blended wing/body aircraft. The fuselage tapers away to nothing, and the canted vertical tails are carried on the widely spaced engine nacelles. The latter have 2D vectoring nozzles, between which are the aerodynamic elevators. The giant wing, of 47·43ft (14·46m) span, has powerful variable camber and at the root the nose radius smoothly increases until it blends into the fuselage, where the gun is installed. Tandem-wheel main gears are inboard of the engines beside the battery of recessed AAMs (in this illustration augmented by Sidewinders on and under the wingtips).

Below: Described in the entry Q in the text, this McDonnell Douglas fighter is one of the configurations being studied to meet the ATF requirement. Related configurations have been investigated with Pegasus-type STOVL propulsion.

Above: Aircraft P (text starts p.53) is a kind of great-grandson of the F-15. To the author the canards plus vectored rear nozzles arrangement has all the drawbacks (eg engine-out safety) of Pegasus-type STOVL without the advantages.

Below: Rockwell International's published ATF (text opposite) looks good, though it is inevitably big with over 1,000 sq ft of gross wing area. Length is 60·17ft (18·34m). Fighters of this size would need engines more powerful than today's F100 and F110.

Bell-Boeing JVX

Origin: Joint programme by Bell Helicopter Textron and Boeing Vertol, USA.
Type: Multirole V/STOL; missions, see text.
Engines: Two advanced turboshaft engines, expected to be based on GE27 or PW3005 and rated at about 6,000shp each.
Dimensions: Not decided, but substantially larger than XV-15, which has following data: diameter of each three-blade rotor 25ft 0in (7·62m); wing span between nacelle outer edges 35ft 2in (9·8m); fuselage length 41ft 0in (12·5m); height (nacelles vertical) 15ft 4in (4·67m); rotor disc area (total) 982 sq ft (91·22m²).
Weights: Empty, probably about 27,000lb (12247kg); max about 40,000lb (18144kg); (XV-15) empty 9,570lb (4341kg), max (VTO) 13,000lb (5897kg), (STO) 15,000lb (6804kg).
Performance: Similar to XV-15, which includes max speed (17,000ft, 5180m) 382mph (615km/h); max cruise 349mph (516km/h); max rate of climb 3,150ft (960m)/min; range (max fuel) 512 miles (824km).
Armament: Various, see text.
History: First flight (XV-15) 3 May 1977 hover, followed by full conversion 24 July 1979; (JVX) expected August 1987.
User: To be USA (Marine Corps, probably Army and possibly others).

Below: In cruising flight the XV-15, designed and produced wholly by Bell Helicopter Textron, is in all respects an aeroplane. This smaller and less-powerful research aircraft is a vital stepping-stone to a future multirole JVX.

Above: One of the two XV-15s (the first, N702,) slowing to the hover over a simulated battle area. It also made 54 takeoffs (five rolling) and vertical landings aboard an LPH, USS *Tripoli,* judged "easier than a helicopter".

▶ Though the USAF and US Navy have for 20 years led the rearguard action fighting against jet V/STOL aircraft, the US posture has been more open-minded when it comes to other types of V/STOL. Now after 30 years of research, most of it at the Bell and Vertol companies, the two firms just mentioned are collaborating in what promises to be a major programme for a tilt-rotor VTOL. It has obvious airline importance as an inter-city passenger carrier able to use city centres instead of distant airports, but its whole development is being funded by the military with the designation JVX, for Joint-service Vertical-lift Xperimental.

JVX is an enlarged derivative of the XV-15, two of which were built by Bell Helicopter in a research programme funded by the US Army and NASA. The XV-15s are powered by two 1,550hp T53 engines mounted in pods on the tips of the wing. Each engine drives a shaft system, interconnected so that either engine can drive the whole system in the event of failure of the other. The reduction gearboxes drive two large propellers which in the vertical mode pivot 90° upwards to act as helicopter rotors. Smaller than rotors, they therefore burn more fuel than a helicopter of equal gross weight in hovering flight. On the other hand, in cruising flight the tilt-rotor aircraft flies like an aeroplane, much faster and burning less fuel than a helicopter. Bell claim that on missions longer than 217 miles (350km) the XV-15 burns less fuel and thus carries more payload than any helicopter, besides flying missions in much less time. It still has all the helicopter's advantages in being able to hover.

The XV-15s demonstrated outstanding reliability in many kinds of simulated military mission, and in April 1983 Bell and Boeing Vertol jointly received a US Navy contract to proceed with preliminary design of the JVX. In 1984 the development was in high gear, with both companies testing the nacelle/wing swivel system, blade folding and other hardware items, along with many mockups of cockpits, systems and payload arrangements. Full-scale development was expected to be ordered in 1985.

The JVX is planned as the vehicle for missions for all US armed forces, in most cases replacing helicopters. The exception is the Army reconnaissance mission, where it could replace the OV-1 Mohawk and RU-21 (King Air), both

Below: A Navy or Marines JVX could perform many tasks, but this is clearly a plain transport such as might be used for inter-ship supply or beach assault. The Bell/Boeing team are convinced such aircraft could operate from small-ship pads.

fixed-wing aeroplanes. For the Navy the JVX would fly combat rescue missions, replacing the HH-3 (Sea King), though it is also capable of flying very effective ASW missions. It can get to convergence zones, where hostile submarines are detected, in roughly half the time of a helicopter, and can fly much tighter MAD patterns than an aeroplane and use a dunking (dipping) sonar system. For the Marine Corps it could replace the CH-46 and CH-53D helicopters in the assault transport role, where fast trucking (often over substantial distances) is more important than prolonged hovering. For the USAF the tilt-rotor JVX could fly combat rescue, replacing the HH-53, and special missions, replacing the combination of C-130s and CH-53s which ran into such problems on the abortive mission intended to rescue US hostages in Tehran. Bell has pointed out that, had 15 examples of the JVX been available in April 1980, each could have taken off from a ship in the Indian Ocean, flown at high speed the 932 miles (1500km) to Tehran, landing on the US Embassy with four crew and seven troops, and returned direct to the ship with all the hostages, all between sunset and sunrise.

Another vital role is AEW (airborne early warning), so visibly absent from the Operation Corporate task force in the South Atlantic in 1982. The basic shortcoming of a helicopter lifting a large surveillance radar is its limited ceiling; the hovering ceiling (out of ground effect) of a Sea King is only 3,200ft (975m). A JVX could, say Bell, "operate from small ships and loiter efficiently at an altitude of 9000m (29,500ft). Radar range tests have demonstrated that the rotor interference is not a problem with a nose and tail radar installation like the one used on the Nimrod AEW".

It is expected that the first JVX will fly in August 1987. As far as possible future production models would use a common airframe, with a transport type unpressurized fuselage with a rear ramp door, and side door with rescue hoist. Clearly the possibilities for role equipment and weapons are open-ended, and one possibility would be an air-defence station carrying surveillance radar and AAMs able to perform the whole task of stand-off interception unaided. Certainly the prolonged XV-15 test programme leaves few uncertainties in the basic capability of a JVX.

Below: An impression of an Air Force JVX engaged in a jungle rescue, protected by an orbiting gunship version. Is this a case of getting ready to win the last war (Vietnam)? Or could such machines really survive in a future all-out conflict?

Boeing USB

It is one of aviation's many paradoxes that, so far, the USB (upper-surface blowing) concept should have found no production application. It is demonstrably the most effective of all forms of integrating engine thrust with wing lift in order to obtain outstanding STOL performance, and is also a system of commendable mechanical simplicity. Though McDonnell Douglas would disagree, many observers have shown surprise at the choice of a different system for the proposed USAF C-17 heavy airlift transport described on p.96.

NASA studied USB from 1959. The idea is based on the Coanda effect, which can be demonstrated by holding a smooth bottle or glass horizontally under a

Below: Boeing's YC-14 was one of a few prototypes that seemed far too good to lead nowhere. Though the USAF just kept on building the much smaller C-130, the USB concept is bound by sheer merit to lead to many production applications.

running tap. The jet of water does not fall vertically from the widest point of the obstruction but, seemingly in defiance of common sense, adheres to it right round the curved underside and finally departs as a single jet from the lowest point. In the same way a high-velocity blast of air across the arched top of a ▶

Below: USB works because of the effect discovered by Henri Coanda: that fluid flow, including air, remains "attached" even when a surface curves away from it. Thus a turbofan can blow air almost straight downwards, giving enormous lift.

wing curves round the surface and remains adhering even if the curvature is dramatically increased, as for example by deflecting powerful trailing-edge flaps. With careful design the airflow can be made to remain attached even when the rear of the wing is curved down through 70°. The sheet of air leaving the trailing edge at this angle has a colossal effect on the overall aerodynamic circulation around the wing, and enables the lift coefficient — the lift obtained from each unit area of wing— to be many times greater than normal.

An accompanying small graph shows how the lift coefficient of two Boeing USB aircraft compares with that of the 727, a conventional transport of roughly similar size. In the YC-14, built for the USAF and first flown in August 1976, two large F103 turbofans were mounted ahead of the roots of a wing that seemed very small for so large an aircraft (much bigger than a C-130, and weighing 100 tons loaded). The whole efflux from the engines was blown out of flattened slit-like nozzles across the wing and, when the flaps were depressed to 70° with the engines at full power, this giant machine demonstrated fantastic STOL capability and the ability to fly (in emergency, not as routine) as slowly as 60mph (96km/h). Like the rival McDonnell Douglas YC-15, the programme was stopped through shortage of money.

Subsequently Boeing (not Boeing Aerospace, which created the YC-14, but Boeing Commercial Airplane Co) was awarded a NASA contract for the total reconstruction of a DHC C-8A Buffalo into the QSRA (Quiet Short-haul Research Aircraft). This involved fitting a new wing with BLC (boundary-layer control) blowing systems over full-span leading-edge flaps and trailing-edge ailerons, outboard flaps and spoilers and inboard USB flaps. The latter are blown by the efflux from four 7,860lb (3565kg) thrust Avco Lycoming F102 turbofans. First flown on 6 July 1978 the QSRA demonstrated even more remarkable performance than the YC-14, largely because a higher proportion of its wing is blown by the four engines, with secondary benefits in greatly reduced adverse roll/yaw following failure of one engine.

Flight testing of the QSRA has demonstrated amazing performance, including operations from a runway only 810ft (247m) long, as well as from USS *Kitty Hawk*. This is despite the fact that the aircraft has a high wing-loading,

Below: The first takeoff of the QSRA after total rebuild by Boeing. A much bigger USB machine (though still based on a Kawasaki C-1, smaller and less powerful than the YC-14) is the Japanese QSTOL, first flown in 1984.

matched to high cruising speeds. In extreme conditions, at low altitudes and with full power at NASA Ames Research Center, lift coefficients up to 11·4 were measured. These are by far the highest ever achieved by any aeroplane in history. Translated into practical terms they mean an attack aircraft of F-16 size could carry a bomb load of 40 tons (80,000lb), or operate from a runway some 656ft (200m) long. All US armed forces are now studying applications of USB for combat aircraft with reduced silhouette, reduced IR signature (because the jets issue from flattened nozzles shielded from the ground by the wing) and with dramatically multiplied weapon load. Fighters are a possible application, with powered USB enhancing lift; other missions include ASW, AEW and COD.

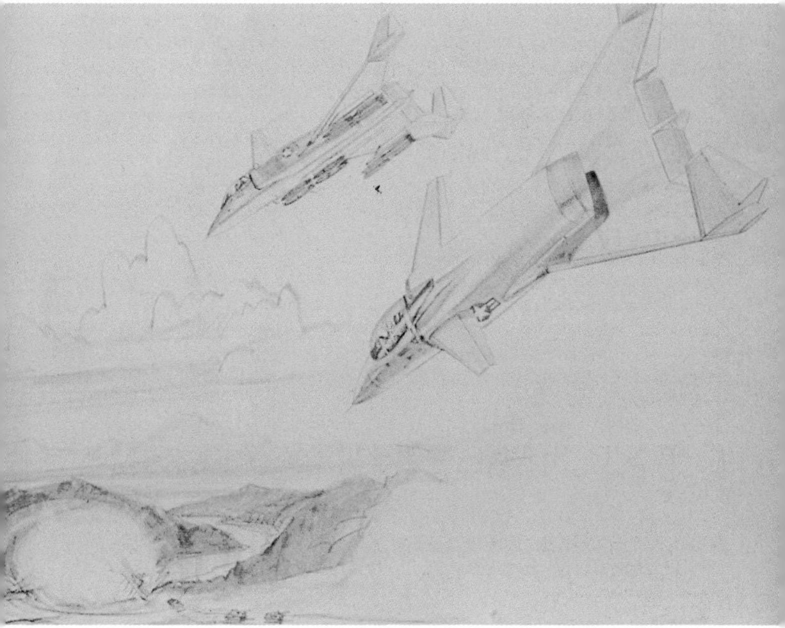

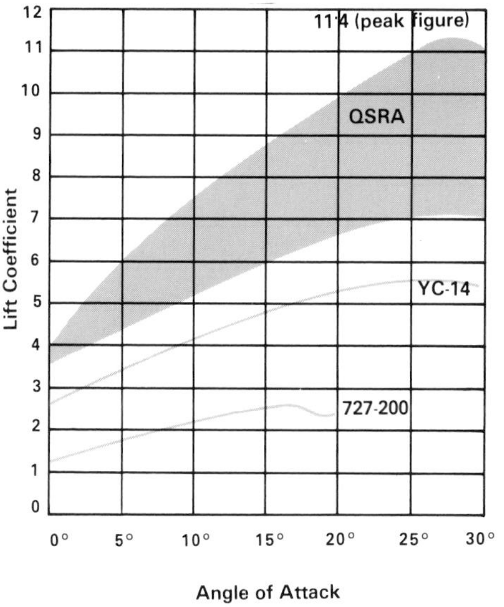
12
11
10
9
8
7
6
5
4
3
2
1
0
Lift Coefficient
11·4 (peak figure)
QSRA
YC-14
727-200
0°
5°
10°
15°
20°
25°
30°
Angle of Attack

Above: Boeing art showing USB applied to a possible fighter/attack aircraft. The single engine blows across the deflected flaps which can move differentially for roll control. Such an aircraft could be amazingly agile.

Left: The staggering results achieved with the NASA QSRA are shown in this plot of lift coefficient for different wing AOA. If the Boeing 727-200 could reach C_L of 11·4 like QSRA it could fly with a quarter-size wing!

EFA (European Fighter Aircraft)

Potentially the most important programme for a new fighter aircraft in the Western world, transcending even the USAF's ATF project, this has a faint chance of going ahead on the basis of most of the European members of NATO. Such a positive achievement in the NATO context would be almost unheard-of, and even now it is wise to avoid being too enthusiastic because of the power of nationalistic interests, especially in France.

The one giant basic step so far was the announcement on 16 December 1983 that the chiefs of staff of the air forces of Britain, France, Federal Germany, Italy and Spain had signed an agreement for an outline staff target for a future fighter. The immediate reaction was a decision by the Federal German MBB company to withdraw from participation in the British EAP (ACA) programme (see below). This is not necessarily a retrograde move, and the ball is squarely in the court of the manufacturing industry of the participating countries to hammer out an acceptable design and an acceptable programme.

What makes the situation so important, and likely never to be repeated, is that the five nations all have approximately the same fighter requirement and the same timescale. The kind of aircraft envisaged is absolutely predictable. Jet lift STOVL is not called for, because all concerned appear to be perfectly happy to put these costly aircraft on fixed airfields targeted by enemy missiles. Two engines are suggested, and a takeoff weight of 17t (37,479lb), including 4t (8,819lb) of fuel and 4·5t (9,921lb) of external weapons. A peak Mach number of not less than 1·8 is required, a structural load factor of +9g/−3g, and a look-down shoot-down pulse-doppler radar and BVR (beyond visual range) AAMs, as well as a gun and the ability to fly surface-attack missions as a secondary role.

The kind of takeoff run envisaged is 1,640ft (500m), which for some reason is thought adequate to protect the aircraft against detection or destruction on its bases. France alone has a requirement for a carrier-based version to operate from the two large nuclear-engined ships to be built as replacements for the existing *Clémenceau* and *Foch*. In all cases a definitive production aircraft is not expected until about 1990, for operational service around 1995. For basic planning purposes it is assumed that Britain, France and Federal Germany will each require 200 aircraft, and Italy and Spain 100 each.

Below: The British Aerospace research programme with the grossly unstable Jaguar XX765 is providing the essential experience with ACT (active controls technology) needed for the Experimental Aircraft Programme described on p.68.

Though the establishment of a common objective by the customer air forces is the essential first step towards a common programme, the next stage is most crucial and difficult. Had no manufacturer done more than private research and study it would be possible to establish a common programme almost from the proverbial "clean sheet of paper", but British Aerospace, Dassault-Breguet, Dornier (in partnership with Northrop) and MBB have all proposed their own design studies, which have been published. The first two companies are well advanced in a programme of prototype construction, with limited funding by their own governments. The objective may be said to be to advance the foundation of underlying technology, but in reality it is to establish an improved political position in the hope that a particular design will be selected. This is certainly the case with the French company, which — while expressing the hope that European partners will join its ACX/ACT programme — is desperate to ensure that the programme is delayed and that Britain does not go it alone.

Early in the BAe project it was hoped that the massive collaborative experience of Panavia would be put to use by repeating the same funding structure (BAe: 40 per cent, MBB: 40 per cent, Aeritalia: 20 per cent) in the programme for a new air-combat fighter. There is no reason to doubt that this would have been possible, and MBB and Aeritalia participated strongly in the design and planning of the EAP aircraft. Having established a viable programme, other European partners could then have joined it, receiving work shares in design and production proportionate to national quantities bought.

This cannot now happen, because while Aeritalia, MBB and Dornier are forced to await developments, BAe and Dassault-Breguet are going ahead with national prototypes, both expected to fly in 1986. The further these go, the more difficult it will be to stop them or merge them, and the more time will be wasted arguing over which should be picked as the basis for a common EFA. The position is made the more serious for BAe by the fact that already there will be what Americans call a bathtub — a period of shortage of work — between delivery of the last Tornado and the first EFA, even if no time is wasted at all. As it is, it is just faintly possible that the participating industries may agree to get down to a common design at an early date, but experience shows that this will probably remain a pious hope. Moreover, existence of the European Turbo-Union RB199, French SNECMA M88 and American F404 shows that we will probably have just as much trouble over the engine.   ▶

Below: The British Aerospace (Warton) P.106 LCA (light combat aircraft) was a single-RB199 predecessor of today's EAP but using generally similar aerodynamics. A major difference was the use of lateral inlets, which are inferior at extreme AOA.

Above: Designed to meet the RAF's AST.414 requirement, the BAe P.110 was the first Warton concept for an ECA (European Combat Aircraft) and predecessor of the EAP now being built. Canard, inlets and tail still had to change considerably.

Below: The first full-scale mock-up of the BAe Agile Combat Aircraft, seen at Warton before going to the 1982 Farnborough airshow. This subsequently became the basis for the EAP air vehicle, which is a technology demonstrator to fly in 1986.

British Aerospace

The chief centre for combat aircraft in Britain must today be recognised as Warton, which after a 1984 structural reshuffle remains a division within its own right. The other great military centre is Kingston, now part of what is called the Military Division. (Manchester, famed for Vulcans, Nimrods and 748s, is part of an enlarged Weybridge Division). Warton is the home of the British participation in the EFA, but it is worth briefly looking at previous background studies.

At Kingston work has centred on STOVL studies (see p.126). At Brough the design team fought to stay in being by proposing a very simple and low-cost LCA (Light Combat Aircraft) which worked its way via the P.159 to the P.163. Rather like a scaled-down F-16 with a high wing and side inlets, this would have had a single RB199 engine and been attractive and cost/effective. Warton, however, looked at the P.103 (see p.126).

Reluctantly, Warton's large project team went along with the general feeling of the customers and dropped vectored-thrust STOVL. It came up in 1982 with two very attractive and exceedingly agile fighters, both with cranked-arrow (or double delta) wings and canards. The P.106 was small, and powered by a single uprated RB199 in the 21,000lb (9525kg) thrust class. Discussions with Sweden, whose requirement was in this class, inevitably failed to lead to a common project, but did lead to BAe Warton receiving the prime contract for the carbon-fibre wing for Sweden's JAS39. It will be noted that the P.106 would have had long lateral inlets carrying the canards.

In round terms the P.106 was regarded as "the poor man's P.110" and capable of doing 70 per cent of the job of the bigger aircraft, for less than 70 per cent of the 110's total costs. The P.110, powered by two uprated RB199s, had a similar configuration except for uncertainty over the inlet location. Studies showed very good results with the P.110, which was designed to meet the RAF's requirement (AST.414) for an air-combat fighter, and this became the first ECA (European Combat Aircraft) from Warton to be the basis of detailed discussions ▶

Above: The final form of the BAe technology demonstrator shows refinements in canards, inlet/Lerx configuration and the single Tornado-type vertical tail. Somehow BAe has to break the French delaying tactics and get a programme going.

▶ with the other partners in Panavia, Aeritalia and MBB. In April 1982 a joint design team was formed by the three companies, and in June of that year the team reported that identity of thought in evolving a common design justified a tri-national collaborative programme. This recommendation was approved by the boards of the three companies, and prospects looked good.

Renamed the ACA (Agile Combat Aircraft), the proposal was exhibited in full-scale mock-up form at Farnborough in September 1982, when it was seen that the inlet had become a sharp-lipped rectangular ventral box, that the wing had shifted downwards and the canard downwards and much further forward. At the last moment the tail was redesigned with twin inclined vertical surfaces, giving optimum agility at high AOA. As far as possible the avionics (including the main radar), weapons and systems were to be based on those of the Tornado F.2, but structurally the ACA was entirely new and the flight controls were from the start of the quad ACT (active controls technology) type now flying in the Warton Division's unstable Jaguar described on page 64.

From early in the project BAe has been supported by such major suppliers as Rolls-Royce (on behalf of Turbo-Union), Ferranti, Marconi Avionics, Dowty, Lucas and Smiths Industries, and by mid-1983 these companies had spent an estimated £25 million of their own money. In addition MBB and Aeritalia contributed to the design process, both in their own countries and at the joint team at Warton. On 26 May 1983, the day before the Paris airshow, the UK Ministry of Defence signed a contract with BAe for the design, development and construction of a demonstrator aircraft to fly in 1986. This EAP (Experimental Aircraft Programme) is intended to lead to the future EFA, but is essentially a British undertaking. While there is no doubt the EAP prototype will fly in 1986, there is no guarantee of anything happening beyond that. Virtual withdrawal of the other two Panavia partners has forced the programme back from two aircraft to one; BAe cannot manage alone on the £65 million MoD input, and in early 1984 requested a further £15 million to get the aircraft flying.

This aircraft will initially be powered by two RB199 Mk 104 engines, probably with reversers as in the Tornado F.2. Estimated span and length are respectively 35ft 8·75in (10·89m) and 48ft 7·5in (14·82m). Takeoff gross weight for the air-combat mission is put as high as 35,275lb (16000kg). This size and weight are very much at variance with the strong emphasis being placed on "affordability, and thus on low cost of ownership". Obviously, the EAP will have at least one gun, either a 25mm Aden or 27mm Mauser, and a mix of missiles including AIM-120A Amraam, Asraam, Sky Flash, Alarm and surface-attack weapons.

Above: Dassault-Breguet's policy with the still-fluid ACX is to demand "project leadership" and a 46 per cent share of any EFA programme. They want to delay EFA until the late 1990s so that they can sell more Mirage 2000s throughout the 1980s.

Ferranti have stated the best radar for air intercept would be the Marconi/Ferranti Foxhunter (as in Tornado F.2), while for surface attack, which might be a separate version of the same aircraft, the choice would be Blue Falcon, as chosen for the updated Sea Harrier. Last-minute changes include small wing dogteeth and a single vertical tail already built in the Tornado programme. Aeritalia may provide the carbon-fibre wing.

Dassault-Breguet
Very similar to the BAe aircraft in size and configuration, apart from the twin lateral inlets and single vertical tail, the ACX in fact appears almost identical to the original P.110 project at Warton dating from slightly earlier. All the expected new-technology features have been mentioned, including fibre-optic digital data highways, and two that might not have been taken for granted: active anti-turbulence ride control and voice command of systems, which were first explored in the F-16/AFTI as described on page 75. Certainly these fighters with giant fixed-geometry wings would be hopeless in the high-speed low-level attack mission without powerful ride control to make the pilot's life bearable.

A single ACX demonstrator is intended to fly in 1986, funded largely by the French government and powered by two General Electric F404 engines. This is intended to lead to a production aircraft in two versions, the ACT (avion de combat tactique) for the Armée de l'Air and the ACM (avion de combat marin) for the Aéronavale, to serve aboard the new carriers *Charles de Gaulle* and her sister. Unlike all other European manufacturers, Dassault-Breguet is not positively seeking to be part of a multinational programme. Predictably it is at present taking the view that it is prepared to have other nations join in, provided that Dassault-Breguet is given clear project leadership, and provided the French armed forces dictate the exact form of the final aircraft and that collaboration does not add to the cost. Certainly, to attempt to get France to participate in a true collaborative programme would be very difficult indeed, and unless the other nations simply give in and act as subcontractors to Dassault there is the prospect of a prolonged waste of time.

The specification for the ACX is very close indeed to that for BAe's EAP. A production ACT would be powered by two SNECMA M88 engines, which have just begun development; the first M88 prototype engine ran in early 1984, by which time 900 RB199 engines had been delivered. Compared with the RB199 the M88 is considerbly longer (150in, 381cm compared with 127in, 323cm) and rather heavier, and the thrust with full afterburner is fractionally lower; ▶

Above: Though it has neither canards nor a horizontal tail the N/D 102 would be an exceedingly agile fighter, and could be afforded by many customers. This Dornier model is viewed favourably by many of the divisive German factions.

▶ SNECMA intend later in the 1980s to make it more powerful, though it is never likely to catch the RB199 in this regard. Certainly it will place no mean strain on the French budget to fund the new engine, and two versions of the new fighter, as well as two big nuclear carriers and an ongoing national nuclear deterrent based on land and at sea.

Dornier/Northrop

Dornier GmbH, of Friedrichshafen, has never shrunk from spending its own money when this has seemed justified. It has for six years been studying what will replace the F-4F Phantoms of the Luftwaffe when, despite their planned major update, they become no longer competitive around 1995. In collaboration with Northrop it has carried out a great deal of research, and unquestionably must have a slice of the action should an EFA finally be agreed.

From the start Dornier has pointed to the sheer numbers of increasingly formidable aircraft in the Warsaw Pact air forces. It has therefore refused to subscribe to large and costly fighter ideas, and since 1982 has refined a low-cost design called the N/D 102. Northrop is facing both ways in this programme, because — though the timing is very different — it must to some degree be a competitor of the US company's own F-20A. Powered by two non-afterburning Pratt & Whitney PW1120-series engines, each of some 13,800lb (6260kg) thrust, it is an attractive machine in the 25,000lb (11340kg) class, with a thin wing with LEX and most taper on the leading edge, but no horizontal tail. The N/D 102 would be neutrally stable or even unstable, with computerized pitch control effected by the engine nozzles and wing movable surfaces. The aircraft would have the low fuel burn of small non-afterburning engines, the simplicity of a tailless machine and the agility of a CCV aircraft with pitch-pointing and direct lift control. The two partners are eager to build a prototype, but are wisely waiting to see what happens in the EFA discussions.

MBB

Messerschmitt-Bölkow-Blohm GmbH, Federal Germany's biggest aerospace company, has for many years been studying advanced fighters. In recent years a reasonable concern over probable costs has caused some diversion of attention towards a light fighter in the 25,000lb (11340kg) gross weight class, paralleling Dornier's studies. The mainstream project, however, is TKF-90 (TKF, German for tactical combat aircraft, and 90 meaning service in 1990). Obviously the

Above: An MBB drawing of their JF90, which is an almost exact parallel to the BAe proposal. Will the other Europeans ever break the log-jam of the French and succeed in going ahead with a multinational development programme?

Below: MBB's CCV F-104 is now engaged in a Phase IV flight programme which, like that of the BAe ACT Jaguar, will underpin a future fighter. Dassault has built no EFA technology demonstrator, claiming this is provided by the Mirage 2000.

timescale will have to be extended, and future delays seem inevitable, but the good news is that TKF-90 and Britain's EAP are now indistinguishable. The final difference was removed in early 1983 when the Warton team adopted MBB's rectangular ventral inlet; indeed, the possibility has existed since that time of the three members of Panavia going ahead on the originally planned 40:40:20 basis, perhaps slightly adjusted to admit Spain as an additional partner.

MBB has carried out a vast amount of research into its TKF-90 design, including making a complete carbon-fibre front fuselage and flying an F-104G (built originally by MBB in the 1960s) with major aerodynamic and flight-control changes in a CCV programme. In the picture it is just possible to see the extra fin and canard surface mounted above the forward fuselage. In 1984-85 MBB was in Phase IV testing with this aircraft, involving new software, backup system and autopilot modes, and a cockpit data terminal. The resulting control behaviour feeds across to the TKF-90, which of course will also have relaxed stability and computerized control. By 1984 Germany had regrettably divided into different factions supporting different ideas, including purchase of existing aircraft; the favoured new-build name is JF90 (Jagdflugzeug, fighter).

General Dynamics F-16 Fighting Falcon

Data for future production F-16

Origin: General Dynamics Corporation, USA.

Type: Multirole fighter.

Engine: One 29,000lb (13154kg) thrust GE F110-100 augmented turbofan.

Dimensions: Span 31ft 0in (9·449m) (32ft 10in/10·1m over missile fins), length (both versions, excl probe) 47ft 7in (14·52m); height overall 16ft 8½in (5·09m); wing area 300.0sq ft (27·87m²).

Weights: Empty (A) 15,137lb (6866kg), (B) 15,778lb (7,157kg), loaded (AAMs only) (A) 23,357lb (10594kg), (B) 22,814lb (10348kg), (max external load) (both) 35,400lb (16057kg), (Block 25 on) 37,500lb (17010kg).

Performance: Max speed (AAMs only) 1,350mph (2173km/h, Mach 2·05) at 40,000ft (12·19km); max at SL 915mph (1472km/h, Mach 1·2), initial climb (AAMs only) 50,000ft (15·24km)/min; service ceiling, over 50,000ft (15·24km); tactical radius (six Mk 82, internal fuel, Hi-Lo-Hi) 340 miles (547km); ferry range 2,415 miles (3890km).

Armament: One M61A-1 20mm gun with 500/515 rounds, centreline pylon for 250gal (1136lit) drop tank or 2,200lb (998kg) bomb, inboard wing pylons for 4,500lb (2041kg) each, middle wing pylons for 3,500lb (1587kg) each, outer wing pylons for 700lb (318kg) each (being uprated under MSIP-1 to 3,500lb), wingtip pylons for 425lb (193kg), all ratings being at 9g. Normal max load 11,950lb (5420kg) for 9g, 20,450lb (9276kg) at reduced load factor.

History: First flight (YF) 20 January 1974, (production F-16A) 7 August 1978; service delivery (A) 17 August 1978.
Users: Belgium, Denmark, Egypt, Israel, South Korea, Netherlands, Norway, Pakistan, Singapore, Thailand, Turkey, USA (AF, ANG), Venezuela.

Probably the most important single combat type in the Western world, with over 1,220 aircraft delivered in the past four years, the F-16 is in service in two basic variants, both powered by the Pratt & Whitney F100-200 engine rated at 23,830lb (10810kg) with full augmentation, designated F-16A (single-seat) and F-16B (two-seat). Since 1983 the standard production models have been the F-16C (single-seat) and F-16D (two-seat) with greatly updated avionics.

General Dynamics has also flown two extremely advanced research models, but before describing these it is worth noting that in early 1984 the prolonged competitive efforts of General Electric finally ended the monopoly of Pratt & Whitney in supplying USAF fighter engines. An order was placed for 120 of the impressive F110 engine, for Fiscal Year 1985 F-16 production, and all future F-16s for the USAF will probably have this engine. Its main advantage is a wider stall-free operating envelope and improved reliability, despite the F100's vastly greater operating experience. In addition the increased power is reflected in enhanced flight performance in all respects, and especially in air combat at high weights. ▶

Below: Three of the regular-shape Falcons which, however, all have different engines. Furthest is a USAF F-16C, ready for delivery. In the middle is the early development F-16 fitted with the F110 (then called F101) engine, now adopted for future production. Nearest is the "cheap" J79-engined F-16B, which looks a non-starter.

Above: Though it was placed second to the F-15E in the USAF search for a dual-role fighter, the F-16XL was judged so good its development is being funded for future production. This is the F100-engined single-seat prototype; all future aircraft of this family would probably have the General Electric F110.

Below: On typical missions the F-16XL can carry double the weapon load of today's F-16s, using conformal or recessed carriage. This XL is shown in an attack configuration.

▶ An F110 of slightly earlier vintage was installed in the second (two-seat version) of two prototypes of a dramatically modifed version of the F-16 called the F-16XL. This was lengthened to house more fuel and weapons, and instead of a conventional wing and horizontal tail was almost all-wing, the fuselage being blended along its length into a giant wing described as a cranked arrow planform. The inboard section extended almost from nose to tail, with 70° leading-edge sweep and subtle camber, while the outer sections were conventional wings with 50° sweep on the leading edge and ailerons and leading-edge flaps. Wing area was increased from the figure given above to no less than 663sq ft (61·59m²). Internal fuel was increased by 82 per cent, and recessed stores locations were provided for 29 major weapons, such as AAMs.

Compared with the F-16 in service, the XL could take off and land in only two-thirds of the distance, while carrying double the weapon load, and then fly a mission over a radius extended by 45 per cent! It was hoped that the USAF would buy a production model designated F-16E. In the event the choice fell on an enhanced version of the F-15, as described on a later page, but the F-16E was described as "so good its development must be continued". The USAF Chief of Staff, Gen Charles A. Gabriel, said the XL had "a future application as a single-seat advanced version of the F-16", and it is generally taken for granted that in due course, and probably after some further refinement, the cranked-arrow F-16 will go into production. Whether these aircraft would be in place of planned procurement of earlier F-16 versions, up to the total USAF buy of 2,173, or whether they would be additional to this formidable total (by modern standards), is not yet predictable. Certainly one F-16E is roughly equivalent in offensive or defensive power to about two of the Brand X models.

The second research version is the AFTI/F-16. The Advanced Fighter Technology Integration programme has already been referred to in the introduction to this book. It is a programme of vast scope and depth involving prolonged simulations and ground research, the AFTI/F-16 merely being the sole flying vehicle. It was preceded by the CCV/YF-16, an early F-16 prototype fitted with an analog FBW system and extra anhedral foreplanes. The AFTI ▶

▶ aircraft also has ventral foreplanes, but a totally new digital flight-control system with many unique qualities. Its three computers, each carrying out 500,000 operations per second, can be programmed at the touch of a button to obey any of four quite dissimilar control laws, one for all normal flying, one for air/air gunnery, another for air/surface gunnery and the fourth for air/surface attack with free-fall bombs. If desired the whole attack process can be largely automated, the pilot becoming a passive observer.

Compared with all previous fighters, the AFTI can perform "impossible" feats; it can suddenly dart up or down, or to left or right, in order to line up accurately with a target, without having to roll into a bank or change the attitude of the aircraft in any way. Alternatively, to bring the gun to bear on a target, the aircraft can be instantly pointed in any desired direction within a cone ahead of it without changing the actual flight path. Thus, for example, an AFTI skimming the ground could tilt nose-down to fire at a ground target, whilst still holding exactly the same height above the ground.

There are very many new technology items being studied in the AFTI programme. One of the more novel is cockpit voice interaction. Lear Siegler supplied the VCID (voice controlled interactive device) at present installed, which has a two-way function. It can attract the pilot's instant attention with standard spoken warnings, or it can accept spoken inputs. Should the pilot say "Set bomb release range at 5,000 feet", the task will be completed in milliseconds, whereupon the VCID will reply "Release range confirmed at 5,000 feet". At all times the pilot keeps looking outside, through the Marconi Avionics wide-angle HUD, with his hands never having to move to any secondary control.

Above: Distinguished by its slim nose, this was the original YF-16 after modification for CCV research: a relatively primitive aircraft, with an analog FBW flight-control system.

Below: The AFTI/F-16 may look similar but is, in fact, a very different animal and can be regarded as the most advanced air-combat fighter flying in the mid-1980s. Sideways decoupled motions are commanded by the pedals, but the pitch-pointing, direct lift and vertical translation use a throttle twist-grip.

Grumman X-29

Origin: Grumman Aerospace Corporation, USA.
Type: Experimental air-combat demonstrator.
Engine: One 16,000lb (7258kg) thrust class General Electric F404-400 after-burning turbofan.
Dimensions: Span 27ft 2·4ins (8·29m); length (inc probe) 53ft 11·2in (16·44m); height overall 14ft 3·6in (4·36m); wing area 188·84sq ft (17·54m²).
Weights: Empty 13,326lb (6045kg); max 17,303lb (7848kg).
Performance: Max level speed about 1,250mph (2019km/h, Mach 1·9); other figures not publishable.
Armament: Not yet fitted.
History: First flight late 1984.
User: USA (DARPA).

Though a research aircraft rather than a fighter, the Grumman G-712, or X-29, appears to provide the basis for a close-combat fighter that could literally fly rings round anything else in the sky. As explained in an introductory chapter, the

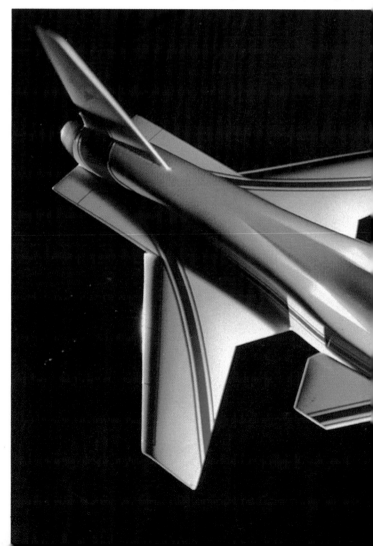

FSW (forward swept wing) offers dramatic advantages in reduced aircraft size and drag, greater transonic manoeuvrability and all-round higher flight performance for given installed thrust. But the two X-29 aircraft combine an entire generation of new advances never before put into one package.

Visually the FSW is the most striking feature, and to be possible the X-29 wing has carbon-fibre (graphite-epoxy) skins with most of the fibre plies angled about 9° forward of the leading-edge angle. Thus, despite having a supercritical section only 4·9 per cent thick, the wing can deflect under flight loads without twisting, and it thus avoids aeroelastic divergence. At the 25 per cent chord line the forward sweep is 33°44', though the centre section is structurally straight across the aircraft and aerodynamically the reverse of the outer panels in being swept back.

A major feature is the use of three pitch control surfaces. The entire wing trailing edge has powerful flaps which also serve as ailerons for lateral control. ▶

Below: This book went to press just before the roll-out of the X-29 in autumn 1984. Unstable longitudinally, the X-29's trajectory is governed mainly by the canards, whose angle is automatically checked and adjusted 40 times each second.

▶ Ahead of the wing is a close-coupled canard foreplane with powerful drive over the exceptional angular range of $+30°/-60°$. With the canard missing the X-29 is neutrally stable, but with it in place the pitch instability is so great that from the first flight the digital triplex FBW flight controls have to be relied on absolutely (there is no chance of adding ballast to achieve stability). In addition large strakes extending behind the wing terminate in powered "tailplane" flaps which give even greater control in certain flight regimes, notably in rotation on takeoff and recovery from a deeply stalled condition. Later General Electric's experience with 2-D vectoring nozzles will be put to use, the new nozzle improving supersonic trim drag, and possibly some aspect of conventional manoeuvrability especially at high AOA such as low speeds at high altitude.

No attempt has been made to achieve very high supersonic Mach numbers, and the lateral inlets are simple. On the other hand the all-round performance and agility are bound to be breathtaking, in view of the thrust/weight ratio and very low drag. Obviously a close comparison with the similarly powered F-20A will be instructive, though the X-29 engine is a regular F404 of lower thrust than that in the Northrop aircraft. In the area of combat agility there ought to be no contest: no conventional aircraft could come anywhere near equalling such an advanced unstable vehicle as the X-29.

The two flight vehicles, backed by a major research programme, are funded by the Defense Advanced Research Projects Agency under a contract administered by the Air Force Flight Dynamics Laboratory, while following initial contractor test flying from Calverton, NY, the major part of the flight programme will be handled by NASA Dryden Flight Research Center at Edwards. This emphasizes the fundamental nature of this research programme,

Below: Like all hand-built prototypes and research aircraft the X-29 has involved extensive hand tooling and skilled detail fitting. Here an engineer prepares the main wing box for bond-testing after assembly, the graphite-epoxy skins being attached to an interior structure of titanium and aluminium alloy. Chalk outlines indicate locations of the joints.

which promises to be one of the most fruitful of the entire US X-series of experimental aircraft.

To reduce costs parts of existing aircraft were used where this did not cause severe compromises. The largest such usage is the complete forward fuselage and cockpit structure, which has come from a pair of F-5A Freedom Fighters. The two gun bays have been used to house the flight-control avionics, air-data system and flight-test instrumentation, the latter alone involving 8 miles (13km) of wiring. The flight-control actuators, landing gears and engine accessory drive system are all standard F-16 items. The engine is basically standard F/A-18A, except for the accessory drive. Later, as noted, General Electric will fit the 2-D nozzle, which will vector through ±30°, and it is also planned to fit a reverser, though whether this will be achieved merely by increasing the 2-D nozzle range of movement is not clear.

Key people in the programme include Col Norris J. Krone Jr, long-time DARPA FSW programme manager and the true architect of military interest in FSW; and Grumman FSW programme manager Robert Roemer and his deputy Glenn Spacht. Spacht considers the very wide spread of research programmes due to fly on the X-29 should eliminate the need for any prototypes in the ATF programme (described previously). In due course the X-29s are expected to be used for research into high-acceleration cockpits, unconventional forms of low-drag weapon carriage, low-visibility paint schemes and radar-absorbent coatings (backing up similar research on other aircraft). What is perhaps sad is that aircraft of this size are no longer of much interest to the USAF as fighters, because of that service's increasing fixation on large answers to the ATF problem, despite the cost. ▶

Below: The X-29 in final assembly at the end of 1983. Though structurally complete the aircraft still lacked almost half its parts by value, including the engine, aircraft systems and the comprehensive instrumentation. It is surprising that DARPA should have funded only a single flight article in view of the unusual nature and importance of this research programme.

Even the little X-29 has jumped in funding and slipped in timing, despite the fact that (in mid 1984) a total of 112 subcontractors and suppliers were either donating or supplying at cost items worth over $8 million for the two prototypes (among them Britain's Martin-Baker, the only foreign supplier, for GRQ7A seats). Originally DARPA hoped to get an aircraft flying in 1982, and for the first two years of the full-scale development the planned first-flight date was late 1983. Then it slipped to April 1984, and at the time of writing was predicted as the third or fourth quarter of 1984. This is despite tremendous enthusiasm and the use of every kind of time- and cost-cutting managerial technique.

Inevitably one gets the impression that the X-29 is not regarded as very important because it does not weigh 50 tons, nor fly at Mach 3. The history of big and impressive USAF fighters, such as the XF-103, XF-108 and F-111 (treated as an air-combat fighter) has been disastrous, and the West might get some really advanced fighters sooner if it took a closer look at the potential of aircraft of X-29 size.

Below: Models of the X-29, or Grumman G-712, have been tested in tunnels both at Grumman and at NASA. Such models usually do not have an active flight-control system to combat their basic instability so have to be very firmly mounted on their sting!

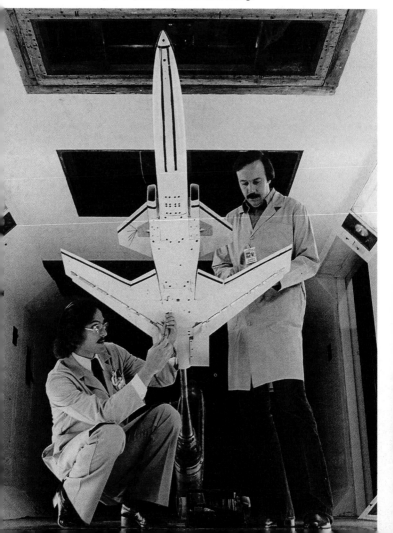

Grumman 698

Origin: Grumman Aerospace Corporation, USA.
Type: V/STOL technology demonstrator.
Engines: Two 9,275lb (4207kg) General Electric TF34-100 turbofans.
Dimensions: Span 36ft 6in (11·13m); folded span 16ft 0in (4·88m); length 40ft 8in (12·4m).
Weight: Maximum 20,000lb (9072kg).
Performance: Max speed 575mph (925km/h); climb to 30,000ft (9144m) in 2·5min; service ceiling 50,000ft (15240m); range 1,650 miles (2655km).
History: Not yet funded.
User: Sponsored by US Navy and NASA.

After unconvincing V/STOL studies such as the "nutcracker" in which the aircraft had a hinge amidships, Grumman began work in 1976 on this improved arrangement in which an otherwise conventional aeroplane is powered by two engines pivoted to the fuselage, and with thrust deflectors on each engine. The nacelles tilt 90° and are so positioned that in the vertical position the thrust lines pass approximately through the lateral plane containing the c.g.

Should such an aircraft be developed the Navy would expect to use it for AEW, ASW, COD transport, SAR, missileer and Marines amphibious assault. In the AEW role conformal radar would be installed, the aerials being along the leading edges and fuselage or tail. No rotodome would be needed, and weight would be 40 per cent less than the installation in the E-2C. The missileer role is one in which the V/STOL carries various forms of sensors and fire control, either to operate its own long-range AAMs against hostile aircraft or to guide large anti-ship or other missiles launched by friendly surface ships. Its big advantage would be its ability to carry its sensors and guidance systems high above the surface at a distance from the friendly fleet, thus opening up targets far beyond the fleet's own horizon. At the same time, so slow an aircraft sitting in contested airspace sending out powerful signals would pose a major problem in survivability.

One of the advantages of the Model 698 is its compact size, much smaller than a Sea King or SH-60B helicopter and well suited to operations from surface combatants down to destroyer size. Grumman and NASA have spent eight years proving the concept, but have not yet been able to fly the aircraft itself. To ▶

Below: An artist's impression of an operational 698-type V/STOL flying over a catamaran flat-top on which also appears a Harrier. The tilting-engine 698 could not fly Sea Harrier missions but is rather a competitor of seagoing helicopters.

▶ save money a 698 would be based on a Mitsubishi MU-2M twin-turboprop, with the original engines replaced by the new turbofan nacelles, a new tail and landing gear, and with the centre section dihedralled upwards. A flying demonstrator would take about four years to build.

Typical mission capabilities would, say Grumman, include delivery of a payload of 3,000lb (1361kg) at a distance of 1,400 miles (2253 km), or delivery of 2,000lb (907kg) of ordnance to a target at a radius of 600 miles (966km) with return on internal fuel, or in a single AEW sortie to sweep 900,000 square miles (2·33 million km²) with conformal radar, tracking 2,000 targets data-linked to the parent ship and with the 300 highest-priority targets displayed in the aircraft.

Obviously such an aircraft would be much faster than the Bell-Boeing JVX, and more efficient in cruising flight, but equally it would be inferior in the hovering mode. Grumman has patented its use of control vanes in the wake of the engines to provide control in the hovering mode in pitch, roll and yaw, the roll control being augmented by engine inlet guide vanes. All control in the hovering mode is confined to the tilting nacelles, with digital FBW control. In conventional flight control is by wing spoilers, the horizontal tail and rudder.

Below: The full-scale model of the Grumman Aerospace 698 mounted for testing at NASA's Ames Research Center, California. This particular rig was out of doors (see below).

Foot of page: Hover testing in the outdoor stand at Ames was done to investigate downwash, suckdown and reingestion of hot gas. The jets were made visible by oil injection.

Above: The full-scale 698 model bears the names of the three sponsors: US Navy, NASA and Grumman Aerospace. Here it is with engines in the cruise (forward flight) position.

Below: In this photograph the 698 model is mounted for testing in simulated flight in the giant NASA Ames open-jet wind tunnel. Grumman say results so far confirm most predictions.

IAI Lavi

Origin: Israel Aircraft Industries Ltd., Israel.
Type: Multirole with emphasis on surface attack.
Engine: One 20,620lb (9353kg) thrust Pratt & Whitney PW1120 afterburning turbojet.
Dimensions: Span 28ft 7in (8·71m); length 47ft 2·5in (14·39m); height overall 17ft 4in (5·28m); wing area 349·8sq ft (32·5m²).
Weights: (Provisional) Empty, about 15,500lb (7031kg); max (clean) 21,305lb (9664kg), (external stores) 37,500lb (17010kg).
Performance: Max speed (clean, high altitude) 1,221mph (1964km/h, Mach 1·85), (low level, two 2,000lb Mk84 bombs and two AAMs) 687mph (1106km/h), (low level, eight 750lb M117 and two AAMs) 619mph (997km/h); combat radius (lo, eight 750lb bombs and two AAMs) 281 miles (452km).
Armament: Four underwing pylons for wide range of stores including bombs, Gabriel IIIAS or other missiles, rocket launchers, gun pods, ECM jammer pods and (inner pylons) drop tanks of up to 561 gal (2548lit) capacity; six fuselage pylons for Mk80 series bombs, to total external load of 16,000lb (7258kg); wingtip rails for AAMs such as Sidewinder, Shafrir 2 or Python 3.
History: First flight due February 1986; service delivery 1989.
Users: To include Israel.

Though naturally protected by tight security, this Israeli combat aircraft — the first to be designed in that country — is gradually emerging from paper into hardware. Though seemingly the very keynote of air-superiority fighter design, its primary missions are close support and interdiction, with the emphasis on the

penetration of heavily defended airspace and accurate delivery of weapons on surface targets. Self-defence does, however, rate high, and with attack weapons absent the Lavi (young lion) should be one of the world's best close dogfight aircraft.

From the start in 1978 the closest collaboration has been maintained with many US companies, which are supplying almost all the major bought-out items (many of which are to be licensed to Israel). At the same time the predicted collaboration with a US airframe partner on both design and construction has been limited to assigning Grumman Aerospace with the complete wing, of mainly carbon-fibre composite construction, in just the way that Saab-Scania has assigned the very similar wing of the JAS39 to BAe. The highly tapered and swept wing has variable camber achieved by trailing-edge and leading-edge flaps with advanced FBW control. The swept canard foreplanes are remarkably close-coupled, actually extending far behind the leading edge root of the wing. Grumman also builds the vertical tail.

The Pratt & Whitney engine is derived from the F100 used in the F-15 and F-16 but has bypass ratio reduced to a level just sufficient for the airflow to cool the casings of the engine. This makes for a smaller frontal area and weight, but at the cost of reduced thrust and higher specific fuel consumption. There is no other application for this engine, which it is expected will be assembled, and partly made under licence, in Israel, by Bet-Shemesh Engines. It is fed by a ventral inlet said to be "based on that of the F-16", but published drawings show an entirely different form of inlet with a sloping multi-shock configuration and a 2-D rectangular cross section with a variable upper ramp. Another unusual feature is that in the front view the main landing wheels are inclined outwards at the top, the reverse of normal; the track is unusually narrow. Some drawings show airbrakes above the left and right rear fuselage, as in many Soviet aircraft.

Avionics is one area where Israel has great indigenous expertise, and the main radar and EW system are both assigned to Elta. The radar, in a down-sloping nose, will be a compact but powerful coherent pulse-doppler type with a programmable processor backed by an extremely advanced distributed embedded computer network which will manage the entire aircraft. The same computer network will be tied in with the flight control system, and also with the EW self-protection system which will immediately locate and identify hostile threats and automatically assign jamming and deception techniques and other EW resources in the most efficient manner. The main jammers will be internal, leaving the weapon pylons available for six Mk 80 series bombs (fuselage) and tanks or missiles (wings).

Left: Though a beautiful example of the artist's work, this side elevation and plan-view of the IAI Lavi naturally contains a lot of guesswork because security surrounding this fighter is in typical Israeli style. It is shown carrying two AGM-65B "Scene Mag" Maverick attack missiles, with two Python 3 AAMs for self-defence. A by-product of the Lavi programme is Israel's involvement in the PW1120 afterburning turbojet. Israel is thus likely to be the launch customer for the proposed PW1120-engined retrofit of the F-4 Phantom, which might become a very big programme involving a number of Phantom users.

IML Addax

Origin: IML Group, New Zealand.
Type: Multirole combat aircraft.
Engines: See text.
Dimensions: (Addax-1) span 44ft 3·5in (13·5m); length 46ft 7·25in (14·2m); height 12ft 3·3in (3·74m); wing area (inc SSA) 543 sq ft (50·45m²).
Weights: (Addax-1) Empty 14,200lb (6441kg); max 46,200lb (20956kg).
Performance: Max speed (SL) 740mph (1191km/h), (hi) about 595mph (956km/h); takeoff to 50ft (15m) 280ft (86m); landing from 50ft (15m) 360ft (110m); tactical radius (lo-lo-lo with max bombload) 480 miles (772km).
Armament: Four 30m Oerlikon KCA or two 20mm M61A1 guns; internal bay for up to ten stores of 1,000lb (454kg) size, plus external pylons for total load of 13,000lb (5896kg).
History: Not funded.
User: Not sold.

This project, and a second-generation supersonic machine of even more advanced conception, resulted from prolonged study of existing combat aircraft to see how efficiently they used their available overall dimensional envelope and how well they could complete their mission with major parts missing. Addax-1 was schemed as a STOL machine with two vectored turbofans (such as the RR Spey or TF34) in the 10,000lb (4500kg) thrust class, and with an SSA (self-stabilizing aerofoil) forming the fuselage between the tail booms. USB (upper-surface blowing), as described on page 60, was to be used over the flaps on the wing and SSA. The Addax-S is a largely different design intended as a supersonic air-superiority fighter based on similar lines. Both machines are configured for outstanding STOL and flight manoeuvrability. The team responsible split up after 1982 and the concepts are repeated here because of the interest they generated. Neither appears likely to be funded to prototype construction.

Below: Though it was not taken to the same point in development as the subsonic Addax-1, the Addax-S had many interesting features and could have used the USB (upper-surface blowing) concept for STOL. Aircraft design could use a few more small free-thinking groups. This drawing was prepared by Michael Badrocke from copyright plans from the IML Group.

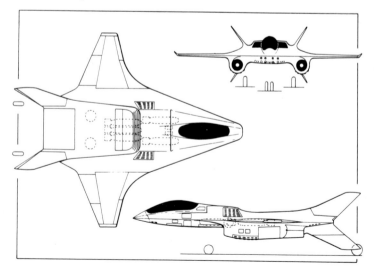

LTV (Vought) V-530

Origin: Vought Corporation, a subsidiary of The LTV Corporation, USA.
Type: Multirole shipboard V/STOL transport.
Engines: Two turboshaft core engines in the 5,000hp class.
Dimensions: Span 58ft 10in (17·93m); length 50ft 0in (15·24m); height 21ft 9in (6·63m).
Weights: Max 35,000 to 45,000lb (15875-20411kg), depending on mission requirements.
Performance: Cruising speed about 400 mph (644km/h); range with max payload up to 1,000 miles (1610km).
Armament: None in most missions.
History: Study programme from 1975.
User: Funded partly by US Navy.

The V-530 is, or was, yet another in the US Navy series of V/STOL "A" series proposals, for an aircraft able to fly many kinds of mission from relatively small ships. Vought has a 30-year history of V/STOL research, most of it concerned with arrangements for lift and thrust from separate turboshaft-powered nacelles. The first series led to the ADAM (air deflection and modulation) configurations of the early 1960s, but by the time V-530 work was initiated the best answer was judged to be the tandem fan. Here a core engine at the rear of each nacelle drives a shaft system which extends forwards to drive two fans each of 51in (1·3m) diameter mounted one behind the other and far enough apart from them to have separate air ducts, as well as a cross shaft enabling either engine to fly the entire aircraft. The picture below shows the separate inlets for the two fans in each nacelle. The entire efflux from both would be discharged at any angle from vertical to horizontal, the latter being the condition in cruising flight. The wingtip winglets help to compensate for the restricted span for shipboard operation, and the wings and vertical tail would fold. The cabin behind the two-seat cockpit would be 21ft 0in (6·4m) long. It could carry troops or cargo, or equipment for ASW, AEW, SAR, amphibious asault and other maritime roles. The programme is an obvious competitor of the Grumman Aerospace Model 698 (p.83).

Below: A V-530 model on test in simulated flight in an outdoor rig which provides a relative wind. The tandem-fan arrangement is explained in the special entry on V/STOL concepts (p.131).

Lockheed-California Projects

Illustrations on these pages show a selection of recent study projects by Lockheed-California Company, USA.

A Seeking the highest combat agility, this unusual parasol-wing concept was found to have some good features. The engine inlets would lie between the wing and the profiled top of the body, the engine nozzles being of the 2-D vectoring type between the butterfly tail surfaces. The wing could have variable camber and, on the outer panels, variable dihedral.

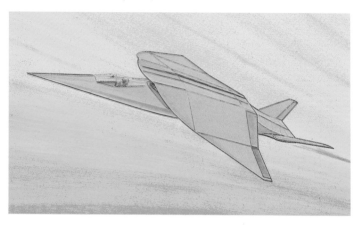

Above: The idea here (Aircraft A) is to increase pressure under the wing by favourable interaction of shockwaves from the nose. It has slight kinship with a Boeing idea (Aircraft B, p.44).

Below: Lockheed is studying water-based fighters chiefly because of the vulnerability of land airfields. Unfortunately most "water airbases" would be hard to conceal, and the parked aircraft open to attack.

B Typical of many Lockheed hypersonic studies, this resembles some of the company's ATF proposals but is even larger, being in the over-200,000lb (90 tonnes) class. The four turboramjet engines have acutely raked sharp inlets with an "upside-down" shape which would probably need variable incidence. The fuselage has full-length sharp chines.

C Resurrecting an idea dating from World War II, and last seen in the Convair XF2Y family of 1953, this hydroski fighter would operate from water and thus, at a stroke, could be dispersed away from obvious fixed sites, and could not be bothered by bombing of its airstrip! Lockheed has studied various wing shapes and ski configurations, this example having a large single ski. ▶

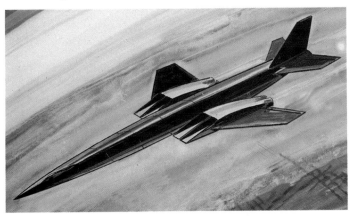

Above: This large and very impressive ATF-type suggestion is described in the text as Aircraft B. The "upside down" inlets are designed to focus shockwaves on the upper lip at cruising speeds in excess of Mach 3. Usually such inlets are scarfed (cut at an angle) the other way up in order to get better tolerance to flight at extreme AOA during air combat. Supercruise fighters would have little power of manoeuvre anyway.

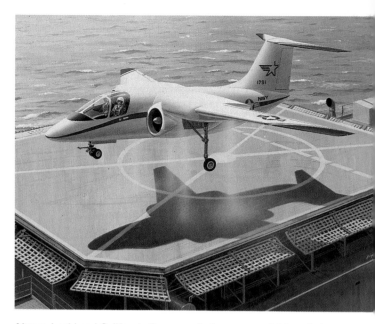

Above: Lockheed-California Company is the source of this artist's
impression (Aircraft E) of a "cross-duct propulsion system" V/STOL for
the USN. A rival to the Grumman and LTV projects, it would have two
turbofan engines with thrust vectoring.

▶ **D** Lockheed has always had a liking for "biggest and mostest" ideas, and it has excelled itself with this, the latest in a series of mother ship or parent platform concepts that have a history going back almost 30 years. Probably nuclear powered, so that it need hardly ever land, it would be much larger than any previous heavier-than-air aircraft ever built, with a span perhaps four times that of a 747. Gross weight would be several million lb (possibly 3000 tonnes). As illustrated it would be the base of operations for fighter, reconnaissance or attack aircraft; about 24 are shown. The turbofan engines would have reduction gear drives to fans of some 30ft (9m) diameter. An aircraft of this size would probably have to be a flying boat.

E Published in May 1984, this scheme is another in the long series of jet V/STOLs aimed at the US Navy for such missions as ASW, AEW, close air support, anti ship attack, EW and mine warfare. Its two turbofan engines have Pegasus-type rotating nozzles and are connected by a cross-ducting system, though this is not explained; it is not practical to attempt engine-out capability with such aircraft except in the purely CTOL mode. The nose-gear towbar shows that catapulting from carriers is envisaged, as well as VL on small platforms.

Lockheed F-19?

Not illustrated, because it is highly classified (as most of the "Skunk Works" projects are in their early years), this fighter is a stealth-technology design with "near-zero" optical, radar and IR signatures. A number, looking rather like a Shuttle Orbiter in plan and powered by two 12,000lb (5443kg) engines, are said to have flown since 1977. The designation is a mere guess, the official DoD numbers having jumped from 18 to 20. Questioned on a recent crash, a DoD spokesman said "I can tell you it wasn't an F-19".

Below: A serious proposal, this colossal "flying airbase" is mentioned above as aircraft D. It is hard not to adopt a flippant attitude to such a concept, and ask, for example, whether the fighters' engines could be used for stand-by propulsion?

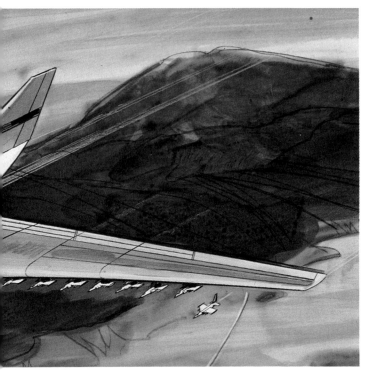

Lockheed MSC Projects

Lockheed Missiles & Space Co is famed not only for its titular activities but also for many RPVs (see the companion *Spy Planes Guide*). It is also busy with other novel unmanned aircraft.

Hi-Spot

This airship gets its name from High-altitude Surveillance Platform for Over-the-horizon Targeting. Funded as a study by the US Naval Air Development Center, it is designed to maintain station fairly accurately at a height of 70,000ft (21336m) for as long as 100 days. Missions include air/sea surveillance, communications relay, sensor readout and other military tasks. It would have a Kevlar/Tedlar fabric envelope with a length of 500ft (152m) and a hydrogen-fuelled propulsion system to counter any displacement caused by winds. Hi-Spot would be unmanned, remotely controlled, and would carry 550lb (250kg) of electronics.

Solar HAPP

Since 1978 LMSC has been working for NASA Langley Research Center in the study of HAPPs (High-Altitude Powered Platforms). A parallel to Hi-Spot, the HAPP would be a winged heavier-than-air machine used in the same way for airborne sensing, long-endurance reconnaissance, monitoring and communications. Numerous applications have been identified for aircraft able to hold station for several days at heights not less than 59,000ft (18km).

Below: LMSC studied the Hi-Spot remotely piloted airship under contract to the US Naval Air Development Center at Warminster, Pennsylvania. The study must have addressed itself to the question of vulnerability of such a platform.

The greatest challenge is the design of the propulsion system. Chemically powered turboprop HAPPs have been studied burning JP-7 (as used in SR-71 aircraft), LH_2 (liquid hydrogen) or LNG (liquefied natural gas or methane). Initial studies centred on small (85ft/26m span) aircraft weighing 3,000lb (1361kg) at takeoff, carrying a 200lb (90kg) payload to about 70,000ft (21km), endurance being measured from passing the 59,000ft level. Work then moved to larger (190ft/57·9m span) machines with electric motors supplied with power by a microwave beam from the ground (which can interfere with RF items in the payload). The most promising results are now being achieved with solar powered HAPPs of considerable size (304·5ft/92·8m span). Studies have been made with solar cells distributed across the upper surface of the wing, and alternatively with them mounted on large vertical fins for higher sunlight capture efficiency at low Sun angles. Gross weight would still only be about 3,000lb (1361kg), and pusher or tractor propellers would give a speed of 86mph (138km/h) climbing to heights up to 80,000ft (24·4km) where upper-level winds are lightest. The central pod would carry about 100lb (45kg) of sensors, immediate applications being concerned with farming and fisheries.

Above: This is the largest size of HAPP currently being studied, compared with an F-14 to the same scale. In this configuration the tail is carried on two booms and there are two pusher propellers on the 304ft (92·8m) wing.

Below: A smaller HAPP, with solar cells covering the fins and outer wings. The latter would be hinged up to catch maximum sunlight when available, but at night would be hinged down for best efficiency, the HAPP continuing to fly on recharged fuel cells.

McDonnell Douglas C-17

Origin: Douglas Aircraft Company, USA.
Type: Long-range airlift transport.
Engines: Four 37,000lb (16783kg) thrust Pratt & Whitney PW2037 turbofans.
Dimensions: Span 165ft 0in (50·29m); length 174ft 2in (53·09m); height overall 55ft 3in (16·84m); wing area 3,800sq ft (353m²).
Weights: Empty 259,000lb (117,480kg); max 570,000lb (258,545kg).
Performance: Normal cruising speed (high altitude) 512mph (823km/h); airdrop speed (SL) down to 132mph (213km/h); takeoff field length 7,600ft (2320m); mission radius (takeoff in 3,200ft/975m with payload of 86,100lb/39055kg, land in 2,500ft/760m, takeoff with same load in 2,900ft/885m and land in 2,000ft/609m) 575 miles (925km); ferry range 5,755 miles (9265km).
History: Not yet committed.
Users: Not yet ordered.

Douglas Aircraft were unlucky to win a major USAF competition with this aircraft, only to have the Air Force have second thoughts and buy more Galaxies instead. The C-17 was the Douglas response to the USAF C-X request for proposals in October 1980. The C-X demand was for a large airlift transport able to carry outsize items which at present can be carried only by the C-5A Galaxy, but which could also fly shorter intratheatre missions, landing on short rough strips and using engine reversers not only after landing but to slow down in the air or to back fully loaded up slopes on the ground.

Douglas had previously built the much smaller YC-15 in an earlier USAF competition to replace the C-130 (in this case the Air Force just bought more C-130s). The company had met the demand for STOL capability by using four

Right: McDonnell Douglas cutaway of the C-17, showing the tip winglets, part-span double-slotted flaps and leading-edge slats broken by the engine pylons. Douglas Aircraft is trying to establish whether a civil market yet exists for such aircraft.

Below: The smaller YC-15 began its flight test programme in August 1975. Here one of the two built is flying slowly with slats open and the JT8D engines blowing into the heat-resistant flaps. Boeing would claim this concept is inferior to USB.

turbofans mounted close under the wing and blowing direct into very powerful double-slotted flaps made of heat-resistant titanium. In the C-17 the idea was taken further, the big fan engines blowing into enormous flaps again made of titanium and using advanced superplastic forming techniques. The C-17 cargo compartment would be 18ft 0in (5·49m) wide and 88ft 0in (26·82m) long, and able to carry Jeeps in triple rows, an M1 tank plus other vehicles, or 172,200lb (78110kg) of palletized cargo. The C-17 would be a highly advanced digital aircraft able to be flown by a flight crew of only two. Four main gears each with three wheels on one axle enable full-load landings to be made on front-line strips, with a 180° turn made in only 80ft (24m). Typical of the C-17's unrivalled capability is air-dropping of three IFVs, the new Infantry Fighting Vehicle. Gross weight is similar to a DC-10.

In January 1982 the USAF announced it no longer intended to go ahead with C-17 production, but Douglas has since continued to receive modest funding to keep the design active and refined to the latest state of the art. It is expected that it will eventually be built, and that production aircraft could achieve IOC (initial operational capability) in 1990.

McDonnell Douglas C-17 Cutaway

Below: Artist's impression of C-17s at work on a battlefield airstrip. It is a prime requirement that the C-17 should have STOL capability, but under ideal conditions the minimum ground roll after landing with full payload is 2,700ft (823m).

McDonnell Douglas F-15 Eagle

Origin: McDonnell Aircraft Company, USA; assembled under licence by Mitsubishi, Japan.

Type: Air superiority fighter with attack capability, (E) dual-role fighter/attack.

Engines: Two 23,930lb (10855kg) thrust Pratt & Whitney F100-100 afterburning turbofans, (E) two F100-200, same rating.

Dimensions: Span 42ft 9·7in (13·05m); length 63ft 9in (19·43m); height overall 18ft 5·5in (5·63m); wing area 608sq ft (56·5m²).

Weights: Empty (A) 27,381lb (12420kg); takeoff (intercept mission, A) 42,206lb (19145kg); max (A) 56,000lb (25401kg), (C, FAST packs) 68,000lb (30845kg), (E) 81,000lb (36742kg).

Performance: Max speed (clean, over 45,000ft/13716m) 1,650mph (2655km/h, Mach 2.5), (clean, SL) 912mph (1468km/h, Mach 1·2); combat ceiling (A, clean) 63,000ft (19200m); time to 50,000ft (15240m) (intercept configuration) 2·5min; mission radius, no data; ferry range (C) over 3,450 miles (5560km).

Armament: One 20mm M61A1 gun with 940 rounds; four AIM-7 Sparrow AAMs or eight AIM-120A (Amraam), plus four AIM-9 Sidewinders; three attack weapon stations (five with FAST packs) for external load of up to 16,000lb (7258kg), or (E) 24,500lb (11113kg).

History. First flight 27 July 1972; service delivery (inventory) November 1974; first flight (C) 26 February 1979, (E prototype) November 1982.

Users: Israel, Japan, Saudi Arabia, USA (AF, ANG).

Since November 1974 the McDonnell F-15 Eagle has established its position as the No 1 fighter in the US Air Force, and at the time of writing almost 900 had been delivered. The first models were the F-15A (361) and two-seat F-15B (58); then in early 1979 production switched to the F-15C and two-seat D with enormous removable FAST packs holding 72 per cent additional fuel without increasing drag, and also providing for what was later developed as tangential carriage for a heavy bombload without occupying the underwing pylons. The C and D also have upgraded radars with programmable signal processors,

enhanced computer capacity, and further strengthened landing gear.

In 1981 McDonnell Aircraft began developing what at the time was called the Enhanced Eagle, and received the designation F-15E. This was intended to be upgraded in the air-to-ground mission, and by 1983 the USAF expressed an urgent need for what it called a DRF (dual-role fighter), able to fly air-to-air and air-to-ground missions. Unlike early F-15 versions the air-to-ground demand was for long-range interdiction with large weapon loads in all weathers or at night. Previously only the F-111 could fly such missions, and a new aircraft was needed able to back up both the F-111 in this task and also the F-15 in air defence. After an evaluation against the single-engined F-16XL it was announced on 24 February 1984 that the choice would be the F-15E, 392 existing planned F-15s being completed as this new dual-role version at an extra cost of $1·5 billion. Production is due to begin in 1986, with deliveries starting in 1988. The F-15E is a two-seater, with advanced APG-70 radar and programmable fire control, LANTIRN multisensor pod, and many other changes including minor strengthening to pull 9g in turns even at incredible weights and with weapon loads up to 24,500lb (11113kg). Compared with the F-111 it has a totally different performance in the air-to-air role, with an M61 gun and AIM-7, AIM-9 and AIM-120A (Amraam) missiles.

Over the years McDonnell has studied various aerodynamically uprated F-15s. A colourful drawing in 1978 showed a canard version in the AFTI (Advanced Fighter Technology Integration) programme, and this surfaced again in late 1983 when the company said it was responding to USAF interest in STOL performance by studying an F-15 fitted with both canards and 2-D vectoring engine nozzles. Tunnel tests showed that an F-15 so modified would have greater usable lift at both subsonic and supersonic speeds, using both vectored thrust and the canards together. McDonnell had previously spent nearly 10 years studying both concepts, and when applied to the F-15 in models and computer studies the results were dramatic. At takeoff the lift on the canards and lift from the vectored jets cut takeoff distance by more than half, while the landing was not only much slower but was arrested by reverse thrust. The company has proposed that a single F-15 be modified to the new STOL high-agility configuration, and there is even an outside chance these features could be retroactively fitted to aircraft already in service.

Left: The camera never lies, but this F-15 photograph has been doctored to show canards and 2-D vectoring engine nozzles. The combined effect would be "a major improvement" in lift, manoeuvrability and reduced drag.

Below: USAF No 71-291, originally the second two-seat F-15B and a much-used company demonstrator, is seen after modification as the prototype Enhanced Eagle. It is carrying 20 Rockeye Mk 20 cluster bombs, FAST packs and four Sidewinders.

McDonnell Douglas Studies

In December 1983 Roger D. Schaufele, McDonnell Douglas corporate v-p Engineering, told the US House Subcommittee on Aviation and Transportation that much more should be spent in the USA on aviation long-term research. He especially noted, "Our largest concern is the relative lack of long-term high-risk research and technology in both NASA and DoD programs". Certainly his own company is not slow in coming forward with new ideas that would cost billions merely in order to fly a prototype, and — unlike the situation that applies in fund-starved nations of Europe — the McDonnell Douglas board are hardly likely to have to pay the costs themselves.

A Though this aerospace vehicle dates from 1970 its shape has not changed much since, though it is no longer regarded as a likely project in the near term. Related to the defunct Boeing X-20A Dyna-Soar, it differs in having an air-breathing engine for use within the atmosphere. It is doubtful that such vehicles could take off conventionally; they would have to be launched like a Shuttle Orbiter.

B Another "far out" project, this time dated 1973 but still being studied in collaboration with NASA, this shows a classical shape for a hypersonic transportation system. Six engines are either rockets or turboramjets fed from a dorsal inlet. Again the problem is takeoff; the Griffith idea of dozens of VTOL lift jets is no longer regarded as viable. A pick-a-back launch from a 747 is a possibility, but not in commercial airline operation.

C This was the same shape dusted off and presented as a "Mach 12 strategic reconnaissance aircraft which could also orbit the Earth more than 1,250 miles high", by Mr Schaufele in December 1983. It was seen that the six engines had been moved to the underside, the profile being reminiscent of a Rolls-Royce study of 1962 which featured external combustion under the upward sloping rear fuselage. Schaufele said "Such an aircraft could take off and land at conventional airfields".

Above: Few would quarrel with the McDonnell Douglas belief that a hypersonic vehicle must be slender and have lots of thrust. This impression is commented upon in B in the text. The company feels more effort should be put into such future ideas.

Below: Referred to in the text as Study A, this was a scheme for what in 1970 was called an Aerospace Plane. Today the DoD is again looking at what it now calls transatmospheric vehicles, the first of which of course is the Shuttle Orbiter.

Mikoyan-Gurevich MiG-29

Origin: The OKB named for Mikoyan-Gurevich, Soviet Union.

Type: Multirole fighter and attack.

Engines: Two engines, believed to be 16,535lb (7500kg) thrust Tumanskii R-25 afterburning turbojets.

Dimensions: (1984 DoD estimates) Span 39ft 4in (12·0m); length (excl probe) 50ft 10in (15·5m); height 16ft (4·9m); wing area 380 sq ft (35·5m²).

Weights: Empty about 18,000lb (8200kg) (a DoD estimate of 28,000lb (12700kg) in November 1983 must be wildly inaccurate); loaded (clean) 28,000lb (12700kg); max (assuming 4000kg weapon load) 36,800lb (16700kg).

Performance: Max speed (hi, clean) 1,520mph (2450km/h, Mach 2·3), (clean, SL) 912mph (1468km/h, Mach 1·2); turn rate at 15,000ft (4572m) (sustained) 16°/s at Mach 0·9, (instantaneous) 21°/s pulling 9g; combat radius (hi-lo-hi) (clean) 438 miles (705km), (four AAMs) 415 miles (668km), (four FAB-500) 374 miles (602km). Note: mid-1984 DoD combat radius figure is ''800km'' (almost 500 miles).

Armament: Six AAMs. These are likely to be of the new type calld AA-X-10 by NATO, with a range of some 30 miles (48km) and equipped with an active terminal sensor. Older AAMs such as the R-32R and R-60 (AA-7 and AA-8) could presumably also be carried, though at a loss in capability. In the attack role a weapon load of 8,820lb (4000kg) is estimated.

History: First flight not later than April 1979; service entry October 1983.

User: Soviet Union. From 1985, India.

Likely in due course to become the true MiG-21 replacement, though for reasons of cost not produced in anything remotely like such numbers, the MiG-29 became fully operational with the VVS (Soviet air forces) in October 1983. Like its larger partner the Su-27, it has many features resembling those found in American fighters of the 1970s, and appears to be a particularly close relative of the F-15, though on a smaller scale.

Though early assessments regarded it as a highly agile and uncompromised air-combat dogfighter, the MiG-29 — known as "Fulcrum" to NATO — is now believed by the DoD in Washington to be a DRF (dual-role fighter), though not in the same class as the F-15E. Conversely, lots of MiG-29s are in service, whereas the F-15E does not reach the squadrons until 1988. The main air-to-air armament is six AAMs, and little is known about these beyond the fact that they are of a later generation than the AA-7 Apex and AA-8 Aphid (whose true designations are R-32R and R-60). The main MiG-29 AAM is called AA-X-10, and is a large BVR (beyond visual range) weapon matched to the powerful and impressive look-down shoot-down pulse-doppler radar. It is possible that this radar/AAM combination is the same as that carried by the much bigger and heavier MiG-31 ("Foxhound"), though the latter is said to be armed with a larger longer-ranged AAM called AA-9.

From the start of Western reporting of the MiG-29 this aircraft has been credited with outstanding manoeuvrability and all-round high flight performance. Though it is still very imperfectly known in the West, all the indications are that it will have as long and successful a career as the MiG fighters that have preceded it. It is probable that it will replace not only the MiG-21 but also other types including the Su-7 and Su-17/20/22 in the attack role, the Su-15 in the all-weather interception role, and the MiG-23/27 in both.

Indicative of the West's vague knowledge of this fighter is the fact that the first drawing of it to be published showed engine inlets under the high-mounted wing with a configuration resembling that of the F/A-18A Hornet. Later a more MiG-like arrangement was suggested, reminiscent of the F-15 or MiG-25, together with vertical tails carried on structural booms extending aft from the wings alongside the engine compartments. But in the very latest DoD drawing no such booms appear; the fins are mounted directly above the two engines, while — though the inlets are moved back beneath it — the wing has moved to the low position! Part of the trouble is probably that almost all Western knowledge is gleaned from reconnaissance imagery seen from overhead, and so the only view of the MiG-29 that may resemble the true aircraft is the plan.

Left: The author makes no greater claim to accuracy in the case of this drawing than he does with the Lavi, but on the other hand it is probably nearer the truth than anything else yet published in the West. Certainly the plan view is known to be accurate in outline, though it is widely believed the vertical tails are carried on structural beams on the outer sides of the engines. The arrangement shown here, with them mounted above the engines, was a feature of DoD artwork published earlier in 1984. Another area of uncertainty is the engine inlet geometry. We show MiG-type scarfed inlets at the front of wing Lerx extensions. The DoD is certain about six AAMs.

Mitsubishi CCV

Origin: Mitsubishi Heavy Industries, Japan.

Type: Research aircraft to underpin new fighter.

Engines: Two Ishikawajima-Harima TF40-801A (licence-built Rolls-Royce/Turboméca Adour 102) augmented turbofans with max rating of 7,140lb (3238kg).

Dimensions: Span 25ft 10in (7·87m); length 58ft 7in (17·86m); height (T-2) 14ft 7in (4·445m); wing area 227·9sq ft (21·17m²).

Weights: Empty (T-2) 13,905lb (6307kg); (F-1) 14,330lb (6500kg); loaded (T-2, clean) 21,274lb (9650kg); (T-2 max) 28,440lb (12900kg); (F-1 max) 30,200lb (13700kg).

Performance: Max speed (at clean gross weight) 1,056mph (1700km/h, Mach 1·6); initial climb 19,680ft (6000m)/min; service ceiling 50,025ft (15250m); range (T-2 with external tanks) 1,610 miles (2593km); (F-1 with eight 500lb bombs) 700 miles (1126km).

Armament: (T-2A, F-1) One 20mm M-61 multi-barrel gun under left side of cockpit floor, pylon hardpoints under centreline and inboard and outboard on wings, with light stores attachments at tips. Total weapon load (T-2A) normally 2,000lb (907kg); (F-1) 6,000lb (2722kg) comprising 12 × 500lb bombs, eight 500lb plus two tanks of 183gal, or two 1,300lb (590kg) ASM-1 anti-ship missiles, and four Sidewinders.

History: First flight (T-2) 20 July 1971; design of CCV 1978; manufacture from early 1979; first flight 9 August 1983; first flight of FS-X, possibly 1988.

User: To be JASDF.

Despite American opposition, because it would mean a lost sale to its own industry (which has found Japan virtually a captive market for defence hardware during the past 30 years), the JASDF (Japan Air Self-Defence Force) is planning to buy a new locally designed·fighter in the remainder of this decade.

At first it was intended only to replace the F-1, but the life of these is now being extended from 1985 to 1991, and the current plan is for the new so-called FS-X — still a nebulous prospect — to replace both the F-1 and the McDonnell F-4EJ Phantom II in the next decade.

Contractors have not been allocated, and it will probably be a collaborative effort, but to provide an essential national expertise and an underpinning foundation of knowledge, Mitsubishi has been converting one of its own T-2 advanced supersonic trainers to CCV configuration. The aircraft, 29-5103, was the third T-2 to be built. The revised aircraft has direct manoeuvre flaps on the leading and trailing edges of the wings, which are otherwise unchanged, and three powerful canard controls immediately ahead of the wing, two horizontal and one vertical on the ventral centreline. These three new surfaces are of carbon-fibre composite construction. They reduce the longitudinal stability to a negative value, which is continuously countered by control deflections of the tail commanded by the completely new triplex digital FBW flight-control system and associated computers.

The T-2CCV is believed to be only the second aircraft in the world to combine digital FBW, control augmentation, relaxed static stability (in this case to a negative value), manoeuvre load control, DLC (direct lift control) and DSFC (direct side-force control); the previous example was the F-16/AFTI. All five flight modes are now being investigated. The aircraft is flown as a single-seater, the rear cockpit being occupied by test instrumentation.

Below: Mitsubishi's T-2CCV is only the second aircraft to fly outside the Soviet Union with unstable aerodynamics, manoeuvre load control and decoupled vertical and side force controls. The rear cockpit is used for instrumentation, and because of the extra avionics the capacity of the environmental-control system has been increased. An F-4EJ hydraulic pump is fitted to each engine to provide the increased power needed by the flight-control system, which is of the triplex type. In this photograph the wing flaperons are down.

Northrop ATB

Origin: Northrop Corporation, assisted by Boeing and Vought, USA
Type: Stealth-technology bomber.
No other data released.

Since 1981 Northrop and its two partner companies have been working at top priority on a totally new bomber which is the first large aircraft (ie, excluding the Lockheed F-19) to be designed wholly on the basis of stealth technology. This attempts to reduce to the lowest possible values the aircraft's optical, radar and IR signatures, in other words it attempts to make the aircraft invisible, to the human eye and to other sensors.

This cannot be realized fully in practice, but signatures can be reduced to well below 1 per cent of what they might be with a conventional design. No hint of the appearance of the Northrop aircraft has leaked out, beyond the supposition that it would have dimensions appreciably smaller than the B-1B and would be of "flying wing" configuration. (The F-19 has been likened to the Shuttle Orbiter.) Possibly to be designated as the B-2, and generally referred to as the ATB (Advanced Technology Bomber), this dramatic new aircraft may have some similarity to the "all-fuselage" Rockwell stealth bomber illustrated on page 17. Of course, everything possible will be done to eliminate aerodynamic projecting surfaces, engine inlets visible from the ground, any kind of re-entrant junction such as that between the side of a fuselage and the underside of a wing, and, above all, any kind of detectable emission such as from engines, radars and communications.

An accompanying illustration is borrowed from another company (Grumman Aerospace) because it is one of the better attempts to give an indication of the kind of aircraft that results when stealth principles are applied. This aircraft has virtually no reflecting of emitting areas when seen from below and in front, and the engines have a dorsal inlet with a large conical centrebody and exhaust through 2-D rectangular nozzles shielded from below and on each side by smooth cool structure. The external paint is non reflective optically, all sensitive areas are covered with RAM (radar-absorbent materials) and the cockpit canopy is designed to eliminate reflective glint.

The size of the ATB project is shown by the fact the initial budget for R&D (research and development) was $7·3 billion. It is unlikely that this will fully cover the cost of definitive flight articles. Facetiously, one can ask "How will the test pilot know where the ATB is parked?" The success in meeting the design objectives is unlikely to be on this level.

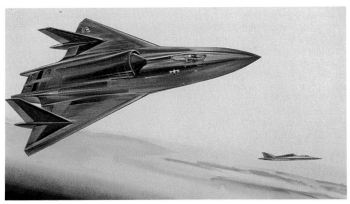

Above: Though it emanates from Grumman this artwork is included here because it is one of the best to appear showing a "low observables" stealth-type aircraft. The side view shows the completely clean underside, with no reflecting surfaces.

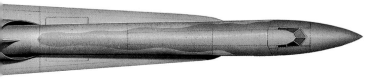

This drawing is pure invention, and is based on a sketch by the author. It does not purport to depict the Northrop ATB, but merely to give an indication of what it might possibly look like. This slender tailless delta shape is obviously a supercruise type aircraft, and we have no reason to believe that the ATB is not a traditional subsonic bomber (though probably with the ability to make a supersonic dash). Unfortunately supersonic flight is normally associated with large IR (heat) emissions.

Northrop F-20A Tigershark

Origin: Northrop Corporation, USA.
Type: Multirole fighter.
Engine: One 17,000lb (7711kg) thrust General Electric F404-100 augmented turbofan.
Dimensions: Span (excl AAMs) 26ft 8in (8·13m); length 46ft 6in (14·17m); height overall 13ft 10·1in (4·22m); wing area 186sq ft (17·28m²).
Weights: Empty 11,220lb (5089kg); loaded (clean) 18,005lb (8167kg), (max) 27,500lb (12474kg).
Performance: Max speed (hi, clean) about 1,320mph (2125km/h, Mach 2); time to 40,000ft (12200m) 2min 18sec; takeoff run (max weight) 4,200ft (1280m); combat radius (seven Mk 82 bombs, two AAMs, two tanks, hi-lo-hi plus large combat reserves) 345 miles (556km).
Armament: Two 20mm M39 guns each with 450 rounds; five weapon pylons (inner three plumbed for 229gal/1041lit tanks), for total load of "over 8,300lb/3765kg"; wingtip rails for Sidewinder AAMs. Loads can include nine Mk 82 bombs, four Maverick ASMs or three GPU-5/A 30mm gun pods.
History: First flight 30 August 1982.
Users: Not yet ordered (mid-1984).

This outstanding air-combat and attack fighter was originally designated F-5G, because it represents the seventh in the highly successful series of F-5 light fighters. Fitting the F404 engine, together with larger wing-root leading-edge

extensions, a broad "shark-nose" and many other changes, has so transformed the all-round performance and mission potential that a new designation has been applied (in the official DoD number series, even though no US customer is envisaged). There is not the slightest doubt that not only is the Tigershark a first-class aircraft in almost every respect but if offers proven trouble-free airpower, good enough to take on any conceivable hostile forces, at lower cost than any other aircraft. Yet, unlike the less-potent earlier versions, the Tigershark has yet to find a customer.

Features include a single engine giving almost double the thrust of the pair originally fitted, a GE APG-67 multimode lookup/lookdown radar with digital processing, a modern electronic-display cockpit, ring-laser INS, and the most modern and comprehensive EW suite. Only the guns are old.

In most respects the F-20A overcomes the shortcomings of earlier Northrop fighters, and for air-combat performance (including surface attack) the cost/effectiveness of this already very reliable aircraft seems hard to beat, but by mid-1984 Northrop had only attracted small commitments — such as four for Bahrein — which did not justify a production go-ahead.

Below: One of the three Tigersharks (No 3 first flew on 12 May 1984) in the attack configuration with clean wings but six Mk82 bombs on the centreline. Northrop continues to offer not only a fixed price but also a fixed spares price per flight hour over the entire life of the aircraft in a customer's inventory. It looks as if the vital sales start-up may come from the USAF and US Navy who need a new "Aggressor".

Rockwell B-1B

Origin: Rockwell International, USA.

Type: Strategic bomber.

Engines: Four 30,000lb (13608kg) thrust class General Electric F101-102 augmented turbofans.

Dimensions: Span (15° LE angle) 136ft 8·6in (41·67m); length 147ft 0in (44·81m); height overall 34ft 0in (10·36m); wing area (gross) 1,950sq ft (181·2m²).

Weights: Empty about 172,000lb (78000kg); max 477,000lb (216367kg).

Performance: Lo penetration speed 600mph (966km/h); max speed (hi, clean) 825mph (1330km/h, Mach 1·25); range (max internal fuel, no air refuelling) 7,455 miles (12000km); field length, under 4,500ft (1372m).

Armament: Eight ALCM internal plus 14 external; 24 SRAM internal plus 14 external; 12 B28 or B43 internal plus 8/14 external; 24 B61 or B83 internal plus 14 external; 84 Mk 82 internal plus 44 external (80,000lb, 35288kg).

History: Original (AMSA) study 1962; contracts for engine and airframe 5 June 1970; first flight 23 December 1974; decision against production June 1977; termination of flight-test programme 30 April 1981; announcement of intention to produce for inventory, September 1981; service delivery mid-1985; IOC (first squadron) September 1986.

User: USA (AF).

Below: The "B-1B" (B-1A No 2) on test over the desert with Aeronautical Systems Division's 30-year-old NKC-135A (No 10 off the line) once used for radiation measures, and later rebuilt as an EC-135A command post but now on air refuelling trials.

The history outlined above shows the unprecedented time it has taken to find a replacement for the ageing B-52. (Indeed the story should be preceded by nine years spent working on the North American XB-70 Valkyrie, a giant Mach 3 bomber that now resides in the USAF Museum.) The original B-1, now called B-1A, was a highly supersonic aircraft, but by 1978 the emphasis was entirely on subsonic penetration of hostile airspace at low level, relying on "stealth" techniques and ECM for protection.

The B-1 features a blended wing/body shape with the four engines in paired nacelles under the fixed inboard wing immediately outboard of the bogie main gears. Though designed more than 15 years ago, the aerodynamics and structure of the B-1 remain competitive, and the extremely large and comprehensive defensive electronics systems far surpass those designed into any other known aircraft, and could not reasonably have been added as post-flight modifications. During prototype construction it was decided to save further costs by dropping the variable engine inlets, which were redesigned to be optimized at the high-subsonic cruise regime.

Another problem, as with the B-52, was the increased length of the chosen ALCM, which meant that the SRAM-size rotary launcher was no longer compatible. The original B-1 was designed with three tandem weapon bays, each able to house many free-fall bombs or one eight-round launcher. Provision was also made for external loads.

A particular feature was the LARC (Low-Altitude Ride Control), an active-control modification which, by sensing vertical accelerations due to atmospheric gusts at low level and countering these by deflecting small foreplanes and the bottom rudder section, greatly reducing fatigue of crew and airframe during low-level penetration.

The B-1B dispenses with high-altitude dash features. As well as refined engines it can carry much more fuel; a detailed weight-reduction programme ▶

Above: Boeing used this mock-up to perfect the OAS (offensive avionics system) operator station. The computer-driven displays (some of which are omitted here) indicate the real-time situation with regard to navigation, hostile threats, on-board weapons, defence electronics and system management.

Below: B-1A No 74-159, the No 2 aircraft, has been serving as the principal development vehicle for the B-1B. It has increasingly diverged from its sisters, but still differs from the B-1B.

▶ reduces empty weight, while gross weight is raised by over 37 tonnes. Other changes include: main gears stronger, wing gloves and engine inlets totally redesigned, many parts (ride-control fins, flaps and bomb doors, for example) made of composite material, pneumatic starters with cross-bleed fitted, offensive avionics completely updated, the ALQ-161 defensive avionics subsystem fitted, RAM (radar-absorbent material) fitted at some 85 locations throughout the airframe, and the whole aircraft nuclear-hardened and given multiplex wiring. LARC has become SMCS (Structural-Mode Control System), and many parts of the airframe and systems have been refined.

Radar cross-section will be less than one-hundredth that of a B-52. The offensive radar is based on the small APG-66 of the F-16, but includes a "low-observable" phased-array subsystem for precise navigation and terrain-following. Most important of all, of course, is the vast ALQ-161 defensive subsystem, which is expected to enable this large pre-stealth bomber to penetrate defended airspace "well into the 1990s".

B-1B development, mainly using B-1A No 2, has gone well despite a hold-up caused by damage during ground testing. It was expected that the first production B-1B would be rolled out some six months ahead of schedule, in October 1984. Deliveries are to be made to Dyess AFB (now home of the 96th BW) in mid-1985, with the first squadron of 15 aircraft becoming operational in September 1986. Ellsworth AFB will receive 32 aircraft from late 1986, replacing 19 B-52Hs, followed by Grand Forks, where 16 B-1Bs replace B-52Gs. The 100th and last aircraft will enter service at McConnell AFB in 1988. Programme cost is put at $28·4 billion (on budget), or about $40 billion including all support services.

Many USAF planners believe 200 aircraft will be needed, and the extra 100 would cost, it is said $10 billion. There is pressure to fund these as B-1Cs, with more rounded fuselages and more complete RAM coatings. The money would be taken from the Northrop ATB.

Below: The fourth B-1A was painted in a camouflage scheme, though a different livery may be chosen for minimum visibility of the B-1B, combined with radar-absorbent surface coatings. Note the long dorsal spine, not present on the B-1B.

Rockwell HiMAT

Origin: Rockwell International, USA.
Type: Remotely piloted agile research vehicle.
Engine: One 5,000lb (2268kg) General Electric J85-21 afterburning turbojet,
Dimensions: (As built) Span 15ft 7·25in (4·755m); length (incl probe) 22ft 6in (6·86m); height overall 4ft 3·6in (1·31m).
Weights: Empty 2,645lb (1200kg); max 3,370lb (1528kg).
Performance: Max speed 1,060mph (1710km/h, Mach 1·6); landing speed 207mph (333km/h); average flight duration 30min.
Armament: None at present.
History: Programme start 1975; first free flight 27 July 1979; Phase I testing completed 1983.
User: USA (USAF).

Two HiMATs are flying, mainly at the NASA Dryden Flight Research Center, exploring realms of air combat manoeuvrability previously unknown. As no human is on board the manoeuvrability limit at present is 12g, which may in due course become tolerable for human pilots after much further research. About half the size of most fighters, the HiMAT (Highly Manoeuvrable Aircraft Technology) has been designed with a modular structure and engine installation so that in future testing every kind of variation and advanced technique can be investigated. Among these are: unstable CCV configurations and FBW control; digital integrated flight and engine controls; advanced supercritical wings; deformable self-trimming outer wings; variable-camber wings; and a 2-D vectoring engine nozzle. One of the HiMATs may be the first air vehicle to fly with a combination of an afterburner and vectored-thrust nozzle.

Normally the HiMAT is carried to release height by a B-52, starting its flight at 45,000ft (13716m). Control is normally exercised by a NASA pilot in a cockpit on the ground, but backup flight control is also provided by a pilot in a TF-104G chase aircraft.

This RPRV (Remotely Piloted Research Vehicle) concept at one stroke enables the HiMAT to make bonecrushing manoeuvres, to test several new ideas simultaneously (which for a manned aircraft would be judged an unacceptable risk) and also eliminates the need for "man-rating" the entire test aircraft and its systems. It is providing an important underpinning of knowledge for the ATF and other future fighter designs.

Above right: The HiMAT parked on the desert at Edwards in its original configuration of 1979-80. Wing flaps are partly lowered but the canards (with sharp dihedral) are at neutral. The main and wing-tip verticals all slope outwards at the same angle. Note the pitch sensors on the nose instrumentation boom.

Right: One of the best air-to-air pictures of HiMAT taken from a safety chase aircraft. Teledyne Ryan, builders of the seemingly endless family of Firebee RPVs, provided the flight control system for this very challenging programme. By late 1984 new configurations may be flying.

Rockwell XFV-12A

Origin: Rockwell International, Columbus Division, USA.
Type: V/STOL technology prototype.
Engine: One 30,000lb (13608kg) class Pratt & Whitney F401-400 augmented turbofan, with modifications as described in text.
Dimensions: Span 28ft 6·25in (8·69m); length (excl probe) 43ft 10in (13·35m), height overall 10ft 4in (3·15m); wing area (main surface) 293sq ft (27·2m²).
Weights: Empty 13,800lb (6259kg);max (VTO) 19,500lb (8845kg), max (STO) 24,250lb (11000kg).
Performance: (Intended figures) Max speed, in excess of Mach 2; takeoff run at max weight 300ft (91m).
Armament: One internal 20mm M61A1 gun, plus two AIM-7 Sparrow AAMs plus various attack weapons, plus wingtip rails for Sidewinder AAMs or Zuni rockets.
History: Contract award 1972; prototype roll-out December 1976; first flight planned for 1979.
User: Intended for USA (Navy).

From 1965 the US Navy was intensely interested in jet V/STOL aircraft, studying the prospects for deploying supersonic fighters of this type aboard the Sea Control Ship and other surface combatants much smaller than the conventional carriers. Spurning the seemingly outdated Harrier, a contract was placed with Rockwell for this extremely advanced aircraft powered by a large and very powerful engine. This was fitted with a giant valve box which, on pilot command, could divert the entire jet to pipes leading out along the wing and the forward canard. The high energy hot-gas jets issuing from complex ejector flaps were expected to entrain 7·5 times as large a flow of fresh air from above. Passing down through the open ejector flaps, this large flow was to provide a lifting force much greater than the weight of the aircraft, while leaving a shape which, once the doors and flaps were closed, and the diverter valve opened to the main propelling nozzle, would be suited to flight at Mach 2.

Rockwell and Pratt & Whitney experienced several major technical difficulties, and despite intense efforts and a great deal of added funding, never succeeded in achieving in the full-scale aircraft the promise shown in test rigs and with small-scale models. It would not be correct to claim that the basic idea of the thrust-augmented wing was discredited, but the XFV-12A proved a disappointment, and funding eventually dried up, tapering off what had seemed a tremendously promising programme. A few teams, including D H Canada, still hope to make it work.

Above: In the vertical-flight mode the efflux from the big F401 engine was mixed with fresh air to provide a much larger and theoretically more efficient lifting jet than a simple vectored-thrust aircraft. Augmenter lift was modulated by adjusting the exit slits between the pivoted augmenter flap sections.

Below: Artist's impression of the XFV-12A. It is fair to sum up this impressive and promising aircraft as a case where brutal simplicity (in the Harrier) proved the better answer.

Rockwell International Studies

In the 1950s North American Aviation Inc was several times the top defence contractor in the United States. Today NAA has been absorbed into Rockwell International, and is some way from being top defence contractor, but the talented engineers are still there, and the fact that Grumman happened to win the X-29 contract does not mean that nobody else has FSW knowledge.

A Though credit for the original research that confirmed the practical possibility of the FSW, using newly available directionally tailored fibre-reinforced composite materials, is due to Col Norris Krone at DARPA (the Defense Advanced Research Projects Agency), Rockwell was aware of this work and was an early contender in the competition to build an FSW fighter. Indeed, at the 1979 Paris airshow any impartial observer might have thought Rockwell had the whole thing sewn up, with the impressive display of a full-scale mock-up (reported by *Aviation Week* as "the Air Force/DARPA FSW fighter prototype") which for the first time brought home the impressive advantages to be gained from using a forward-swept wing. Rockwell's mock-up — for that is all it was — was pretty much an F-16 reconfigured to use an FSW and destabilizing canard. Had it been built it would probably have outperformed other fighters of its generation.

B Back in 1979 Rockwell drew this "strategic FSW aircraft" to show that possibly the forward-swept wing is not restricted to short-range fighters. Seen from the mid-1980's it is easy to fault, because it has virtually no stealth characteristics and is hardly the best shape for a low-level penetrator. It is included here to illustrate what the biggest defence contractors were thinking about at the start of the decade.

C This impression of a large strategic-type penetrator of the next decade is captioned merely "a laser aircraft in flight". Everybody knows that both the USAF and Soviets have flown lasers of impressive power, but how on earth could a slow big-winged machine of this configuration hope to survive in hostile airspace in the 1990s? Apparently a bomber, it is equipped with a World War II style rear turret housing a high-power laser which in this imaginative picture is

Below: Rockwell International got a lot of media coverage from their FSW mock-up in 1979 but lost out to Grumman in the programme for hardware. The canards are backswept and close-coupled to the wing, in sharp contrast to today's X-29.

Right: Merely captioned as "A laser aircraft in flight" this fanciful painting shows that bomber defensive gun turrets are probably far from outdated, though the bullets will travel at the speed of light and have no discernible gravity drop!

destroying an enemy aircraft (presumably an interceptor). Obvious questions are: how did such a subsonic monster get this far in the first place? Why did the enemy interceptor get so close that it came within a simple line-of-sight aim by a laser? Having posed these questions, the fact must be faced that, in aircraft of a different character, high-power lasers are likely to become major weapon systems. Some have been tested on Boeing NKC-135As of USAF Aeronautical Systems Division, in the course of which trials unmanned RPV targets have been destroyed or incapacitated.

Above: This Rockwell suggestion of 1979 is discussed in the text as aircraft B. Little was known in 1979 about the interactions between canard foreplanes and wings when both were of FSW type, and the great distance between the two is here countered by the fact that the engines could easily get into the wake of the canards at high AOA. The inlets look subsonic.

Saab Grypen JAS 39

Origin: Saab-Scania AB, Sweden.
Type: Multirole fighter.
Engine: One 18,000lb (8165kg) thrust Volvo Flygmotor RM12 augmented turbofan (licensed variant of GE F404).
Dimensions: Span 26ft 3in (8·0m); length 45ft 11in (14·0m); no others released.
Weights: The only figure is "normal max 17,645lb (8000kg)", which clearly means fighter mission, clean.
Performance: Max speed (hi) about 1,320mph (2124km/h Mach 2), (SL) supersonic; required field length 3,280ft (1000m).
Armament: One 27mm Mauser BK27 gun; four wing pylons for RB71 Sky Flash AAMs, RBS15F anti-ship missiles or various other attack loads; wingtip rails for RB24 Sidewinder AAMs; max weapon load not given.
History: First flight to be 1987.
User: To be Sweden.

Sweden's strict neutrality has severely restricted exports of Swedish combat aircraft, but the qualities of the next-generation machine in this category are such that the world will probably beat a path to Saab-Scania's door. While lacking nothing in mission performance and versatility, it will be the smallest of all new fighters now being built, and its costs will be correspondingly affordable. The Saab 2110 Grypen (Griffin) (air force JAS 39) gets its designation from J (Jakt, fighter), A (Attack) and S (Spaning, reconnaissance).

Saab has had to tread a careful path betwen running too high a risk and failing to create an aircraft technically advanced enough to remain competitive into the 21st century. For example much of the airframe will be made of high-strength composites, and British Aerospace is the chief subcontractor for the wing, largely of carbon-fibre construction and provided with powered leading and trailing surfaces for maximum combat agility.

In conjunction with the fully powered swept canard foreplanes this wing should give combat agility surpassing that of any aircraft flying in 1984, as well as the ability to operate safely, in the worst winter weather, from rough airstrips, highways and dirt roads. A further requirement for all Swedish military ▶

Below: Drawn specially for this book, this artwork shows a JAS 39 configured for an anti-ship mission with two Saab Bofors Missile Corporation RBS 15F on the inner pylons and two RB24/AIM-9L Sidewinder AAMs for self-defence. Some details may change by the time such an aircraft can be seen "in the flesh" but the basic design is now firm and the prototype is beginning to materialise. British Aerospace provide the main wing.

▶ equipment is that front-line servicing is handled by short-service conscript personnel, so everything has to be reliable and foolproof.

The cockpit will of course be totally new, with a Martin-Baker S10LS seat, diffractive-optics HUD and three electronic displays, reprogrammable by the pilot to show just the items he needs at each point in the mission. Other features include fly-by-wire controls (tested in a Viggen), rear-fuselage airbrakes, plain lateral engine inlets, Ferranti/Ericsson multimode radar and pod-mounted FLIR (which together handle the reconnaissance mission, apart from pod-mounted optical cameras), and extremely comprehensive internal and external EW systems, with comprehensive jamming and dispensing capability.

Five prototypes are being built, and the inventory programme is at present 140 aircraft, of which about 25 are expected to be tandem dual two-seaters. All are to be delivered before 2000.

Below: As it is later in conception than that of any existing fighter, the flight-deck display system for the JAS 39 will be the most advanced yet seen. There will be four conventional dial instruments, each for back-up to the three HDDs (head-down displays) and the holographic wide-angle HUD, depicted in an en route mode at Mach 0·7 low level. The left HDD replaces normal flight instruments, the centre HDD shows a computer-generated map of the local area and the right HDD a multisensor display normally fed with information from the radar and FLIR (or other inputs).

Above: The Volvo Flygmotor RM12 is an uprated version of the General Electric F404 augmented turbofan here seen on a test run with full afterburner. This two-spool engine has already shown excellent stall tolerance and high reliability.

Below: Models of the JAS 39 in its two main configurations. The upper aircraft is carrying four RB71 (BAe Sky Flash) monopulse radar AAMs in the stand-off interception mission. The lower has two RBS 15F anti-ship cruise missiles and either tanks or ECM.

Sukhoi Su-27 (Flanker)

Origin: The OKB of Pavel O. Sukhoi, Soviet Union.
Type: Long-range multirole fighter.
Engines: Two augmented turbofans each in 29,000lb (12700kg) thrust class.
Dimensions: (estimated) Span 45ft 11in (14m); length (excl probe) 67ft 3in (20·5m); height overall 19ft 8in (6m); wing area 690sq ft (64m²).
Weights: (estimated) Empty 33,000lb (15000kg); internal fuel 14,330lb (6500kg); loaded (air-to-air missiion) 49,600lb (22500kg), (max, surface attack) 77,200lb (35000kg).
Performance: (estimated) max speed (hi, air-to-air mission) 1,350kt (DoD figure, converting to 1,555mph/2500km/h, Mach 2·35); combat radius (air-to-air mission) 715 miles (1150km).
Armament: Eight AAMs of various types including AA-X-10; probably at least one internal gun.
History: First flight probably about 1976; production initiation 1983.
User: Soviet Union.

Though Sukhoi himself has long been dead, his OKB obviously remains a source of brilliant combat-aircraft expertise, and nothing demonstrates this so well as the Su-27. This superb twin-engine fighter appears to have been

influenced by the USAF F-15, using MiG-29 aerodynamics but on a larger scale.

Despite its size, accepted in order to achieve long mission radius with many weapons, giving great persistence in air combat, the Su-27 is considered to be able to outfly the MiG-29, which itself was designed to beat the F-14, F-15, F-16 and F-18 in close combat (and is generally accepted as doing so, the F-16 being the most difficult opponent in these circumstances). It is difficult to win by copying, and there is no question that the Soviet designers have carefully studied the US fighters before drawing the first line on paper, but the US fighters are probably unable to stay with the Su-27, which has the advantage of being started when the F-14 and F-15 were already flying. The Su-27 has a completely new pulse-doppler multimode radar with the greatest possible performance against low-flying targets.

What is more serious is the Su-27's armament. Not only is it now estimated that this fighter carries eight AAMs, but they are partly or wholly of the AA-X-10 type. This is the first Soviet AAM which, in its radar-guided version, has its own active seeker. Thus it can be fired against a distant hostile aircraft in the desired "fire and forget" manner, the Su-27 then either engaging other targets or turning away. There is no need to keep flying towards the enemy in order to illuminate the target with the fighter's own radar. The X-10 flies on strapdown inertial guidance until its own active radar switches on and locks-on to the target. This capability will not arrive in Western squadrons until the AIM-120A (Amraam) becomes operational in, it is hoped, 1986. The Soviet X-10 is part of the Su-27 weapon system which is already in preliminary service and was expected to be declared operational in Spring 1984. It includes an IR search/track system and magnifying optics.

The aircraft itself has a blended wing/body form, and as the inlets cannot be seen from above because of the long leading-edge root extensions they are largely speculative. The wing is well aft, the fins are vertical and overlap the wing and tailplanes, and the latter do not extend aft of the nozzles as in the MiG-29. The tailplanes are probably roll-control tailerons.

There is probably a tandem two-seat Su-27, and a reconnaissance pod or pallet can be carried. This aircraft is reported by the DoD to be in production at Komsomolsk, in the Far East.

Left: This is believed to be the most convincing illustration of the Su-27 yet to appear in the West, but Soviet aircraft can never be taken for granted. The US Department of Defense gives the standard air interception armament as "eight AAMs", but it has not elaborated on whether all eight can be of the large medium-range type (so-called AA-7 Apex are shown here on four wing pylons, with close-range AA-8 Aphid on the outboard rails). In this illustration conventional bombs are shown in conformal stations along the flanks of the fuselage, as on the F-15, but this is speculative. Indeed, no information is yet available regarding attack loads, though the Su-27 has always been described as a multirole fighter, denoting an attack capability. A tank is shown on the centreline.

Supersonic V/STOLs

Once jet V/STOL had been demonstrated in the 1950s there was a great upsurge of interest in 1959-63 because of its unique possibilities. At a small penalty in aircraft weight and cost — typically 15 per cent — compared with a CTOL long-runway aircraft, it opens up the unique possibility of needing no airfield or carrier. Instead, such aircraft can operate from so many small clearings, ship pads, mobile platforms and Skyhook-type hinged arms that no pre-emptive strike could eliminate more than a small fraction of the force.

There has been prolonged resistance to the acceptance of no-airfield aircraft, but fortunately the basic technology of jet V/STOL has never totally ground to a halt, and today several alternative schemes are being explored — haltingly, on near-zero budgets — so that, with luck, they will be developed by the time the decision-takers wake up to the fact that airfields are untenable, except in peacetime.

Vectored thrust with PCB

Kingston, the centre responsible for the Harrier, has naturally concentrated on jet STOVL. The stumbling-block has been absence of an RAF AST (Air Staff Target), other than the basic need for a second-generation Harrier now met by the Harrier GR.5. But studies have never stopped, and one is illustrated. The P.1214-3 typifies the recent thinking of the former Hawker team in combining the unique basing versatility and other attributes of the Harrier with supersonic speed and in-flight agility second to none. An FSW (forward-swept wing) design, it would have a plain ventral inlet to a Pegasus with three nozzles, the hot jet issuing from a single nozzle on the centreline. All nozzles would have PCB or reheat. Aerodynamic and structural problems would be generally very unusual, but this aircraft would have the enormous advantage over non-STOVL rivals that the enemy could never catch it on the ground.

At Warton there have been many technically very interesting studies. The P.103 was one of the suggestions to meet the stillborn AST.403 to find a replacement for Warton's own Jaguar. A substantial canard single-seater, its twin afterburning RB199 engines were hung on pivots so that STOVL capability equalled that of the Harrier. The proposal got as far as a full-scale mock-up, with

Below; Next step in V/STOL (or rather STOVL) technology is the vectored-thrust engine with plenum-chamber burning (PCB). This engine, a simplified successor to the Pegasus with the emphasis on few parts and light weight, has one rear nozzle.

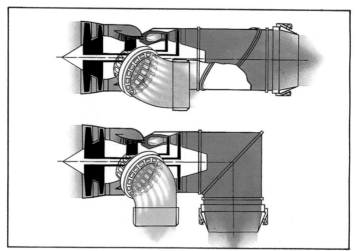

tandem Sky Flash AAMs under the fuselage. In most respects this configuration was impressive, but nobody could solve the problem of how to lose an engine in the vertical lift mode and save the aircraft. This 1980-81 project was discussed with European partners and, in 1981, with Saudi Arabia, but despite its attractions was a non-starter.

Above: Rivalry from Warton will probably prevent further development, but the British Aerospace P.1214-3 could be the most manoeuvrable aircraft ever built. The rear jet could develop favourable circulation around the inner wings.

Below: While it is discussed in the text on these pages, the BAe P.103 uses the tilting-nacelle or pivoted-engine technique dealt with on pages 132-133. Rolls-Royce and BAe have worked on a scheme for using the main engines for aircraft control.

▶ **McDonnell Douglas Model 279**

Origin: McDonnell Aircraft Company, USA.
Type: STOVL fighter (data for 279-3).
Engine: One 36,900lb (16738kg) thrust Rolls-Royce Pegasus 11-33B or derived vectored-thrust PCB turbofan.
Dimensions: Span 36ft 10·8in (11·25m); length 56ft 0in (17·07m); height 17ft 4in (5·29m).
Weights: Empty about 16,000lb (7258kg), max about 30,000lb (VTO) or 35,000lb (15876kg).
Performance: Max speed Mach 2 (1,320mph, 2125km/h), clean at height; acceleration from Mach 0·8 to 1·6 in 70s; strike radius (max weapon load) about 330 miles (531km) lo-lo-hi.
Armament: Undecided but will probably include an internal gun; up to 18,000lb (8165kg) external weapon load for STO run of 400ft (122m).
History: Studied from 1979.
User: Not yet funded but of interest to the US Navy.

The most likely next-generation follow-on to the AV-8B Harrier II is a close-coupled supersonic canard being developed by McDonnell Aircraft with tunnel assistance by NASA Ames Research Center. More than 25 years earlier, NASA Langley had been of crucial assistance in the early days of the Hawker P.1127, from which all these aircraft are descended.

Much depends on the engine, and with MoD(PE) funding Rolls-Royce is at last making progress with PCB (plenum-chamber burning) which is the concept of afterburning as applied to a vectored thrust turbofan. Extra fuel burned in the front nozzles greatly boosts thrust, and makes the engine suitable for the propulsion of highly supersonic aircraft.

It is fair to say that anyone who really knows anything about the subject is convinced that future vectored-thrust combat aircraft will always take off with an STO run, unless this is impossible for any reason; but whether the landing should be a VL is less certain. Even at light weight a VL would probably demand PCB, and much remains to be done to clear PCB engines for landing at zero forward speed. In the Model 279-3 the engine is fed via supersonic variable

Below: A hot-gas tunnel model of the McDonnell Douglas 279-4, a larger twin-engined V/STOL with left and right handed PCB Pegasus engines. Such a model can measure flow, circulation, temperature distribution, reingestion and achieved lift or thrust.

lateral inlets and discharges through four nozzles (in contrast to the 'three-poster' idea in vogue in 1979). The relative positions of the engine and inner wing, with flaps, is based on the Harrier II, but the flow pattern is modified by the canard and, more strongly, by the PCB and low position of the front nozzles which are very reminiscent of those of the PCB BS.100 engine of 1963. Discharging the fan air diagonally out and down to front nozzles at the "5 and 7 o'clock" positions, seen from the front, not only avoids scrubbing of the supersonic hot jets over any rear nozzles downstream but also causes the front jets to impinge on each other close below the aircraft, avoiding a hot rising fountain in low hovering.

McDonnell have no funds yet to build a 279-3, but the outlook is very promising. Meanwhile a photograph shows a tunnel model of the larger twin-engined 279-4, with two advanced PCB Pegasus with handed (left and right) nozzle systems.

Above: With a lot of technology input from BAe and Rolls-Royce, as well as its sponsor, the McDonnell Douglas Model 279-3 is the most refined of all the next-generation projects to succeed the Harrier family. An advanced supersonic aircraft slightly larger than a Harrier (but much greater in wing-plus-canard area) it would have a single PCB engine of basic Pegasus type and could fly almost any kind of combat mission.

RALS

The remote augmented lift system takes the air ejected through the front nozzles of a normal VT (vectored thrust) turbofan and pipes it to a remote lift nozzle near the nose. Thus the main engine(s) can be nearer the tail, and the aircraft takes on a more normal appearance without nozzles amidships.

The advantages are; the aircraft configuration is better suited to supersonic flight; in forward flight the propulsion system is almost conventional, the inlets leading to a conventional engine with straight-through flow; the installation of an afterburner is facilitated; the single remote lift nozzle can be fitted with an efficient PCB-type combustion system to boost thrust, with fewer restrictions on curvature, total envelope size and need for vectoring. The drawbacks are: the weight and bulk of the air pipe and internal remote nozzle; the need for controllable doors in the fan delivery duct to divert the entire flow to the RALS when necessary; possible loss in lift resulting from removal of the rear nozzles from the proximity of the wing where they can induce highly favourable circulation; the need for a major transfer of flow during transition; the fact that high-weight STO ski takeoffs are impossible; and, compared with Harrier-type aircraft, loss in flexibility because of the slow-acting cumbersome nature of the RALS which cannot be used as an aid to dogfight manoeuvrability. ▶

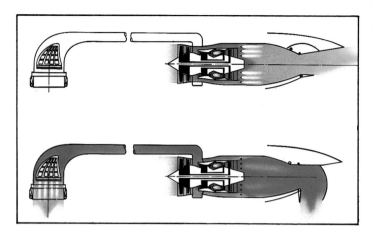

Above: RALS (remote augmented lift system) is described on the preceding page. In the cruise regime (upper), engine performance is uncompromised with straight-through flow. For vertical flight fan air is bled to a PCB nozzle near the nose of the aircraft.

▶ **EL**

Ejector lift is a near-relative of RALS which has the advantage of having been extensively explored in the Lockheed XV-4A Hummingbird in a US Army programme terminated in 1964. The fan air is diverted to a row of primary nozzles in a large vertical ejector duct in the fuselage, with doors above and below. The high-speed (possibly supersonic) jets blasting downwards from these small holes or slits not only provide lift but also entrain a much greater flow of fresh air through the duct. This increases lift by more than 70 per cent, and at the same time, by lowering mean jet velocity and temperature, greatly eases problems of erosion and reingestion in hovering near the ground. Compared with the Harrier's Pegasus, an EL engine would need a fan with

Below: The EL (ejector lift) scheme is a variation on RALS which attempts to gain increased efficiency in the vertical lift mode by entraining a large extra flow of fresh air through the lift duct. Fan air, which normally feeds an afterburner jet in supersonic flight, is diverted to a row of nozzles in the lift duct. Inevitably this duct compromises design of the fighter.

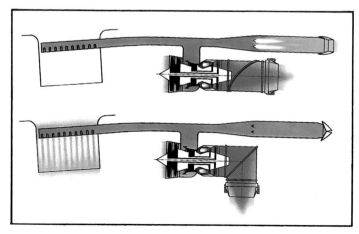

higher pressure ratio to reduce the size of the duct and ejector. (The ideal engine is almost identical to that best suited to RALS and to PCB with side nozzles).

Most important of current EL fighters is the General Dynamics E-series, which encompass at least eight configurations. The E-7 has a single GE F110 engine and an airframe derived from the F-16 but with tailless delta aerodynamics. It was intended as a Navy DLI (deck-launched intercept) fighter, and is currently the subject of a NASA tunnel programme. It will be seen that in forward flight the fan air is switched from the ejector to a separate propulsive nozzle which for supersonic acceleration incorporates an afterburner. There is some affinity between EL and the system used in the XFV-12A.

Tandem fan
The main drawback of the simple VT engine, compared with a helicopter or other V/STOL system, is that it operates with a relatively small airflow ejected with high energy. To reduce hovering fuel burn, as well as nose/erosion/reingestion problems, it is necessary to increase the total airflow, and in this scheme (patented by Rolls-Royce in various forms in 1975) there are two inlets to the one engine. In the hovering mode both are open, the one at the front admitting air through the front fan which goes straight out through a vertical PCB front nozzle. The core takes air from the second inlet. In forward flight this second inlet is closed, the transverse shut-off valve is opened and the engine becomes a (rather long) augmented turbofan with straight-through flow.

Obviously it is rather cumbersome compared with, say, an RB199 (on which the current core studies are based), but against this must be set the significantly reduced fuel burn in vertical flight, to the extent that it has been found possible to reduce total mission fuel by using both inlets and nozzles in subsonic cruise and loiter parts of the mission. One company which arrived at the TF layout independently was Vought, via ADAM studies (see page 89). The Vought TF-120 is a modern study for a DLI fighter with potentially outstanding performance. The auxiliary inlet is in the top of the fuselage.

Hybrid fan
A close relative of the tandem fan, this is externally a simple VT engine of the three-poster type. Thus it can be used with a single cockpit nozzle angle lever for any kind of takeoff from vertical to conventional, including a ski jump. ▶

Below: Another scheme, being explored by Vought, is the tandem fan. In high-speed flight the only odd thing is the wide longitudinal separation of the first and second fan stages, but in the vertical lift regime these stages are completely separated by a valve. The first stage feeds a lift jet at the front while the second draws air through an auxiliary inlet to feed the core.

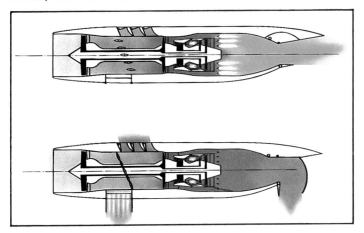

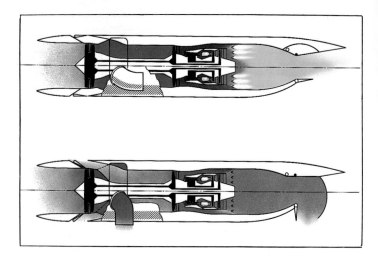

Above: Though Rolls-Royce believe the tandem fan shows most promise of reducing the so-called penalties of jet lift to a minimum, the hybrid fan shown here is running it very close and is showing increasing promise as the geometry is refined.

▶ Internally it has the advantage of separating the front fan flow from the core when necessary, at the cost of a rather complicated valve arrangement. Despite this, Rolls-Royce regard it as likely to become one of the best future V/STOL propulsion systems, and is engaged in studies for the US Navy on both the HF and TF concepts. Indeed, certainly for shipboard operation where erosion is no problem, the signs are that a refined TF/HF system will prove the best answer of all for supersonic V/STOLs of the 1990s.

Lift jets

Largely because of the respect commanded by Rolls-Royce, which ardently championed it, the use of the battery of separate lift engines was the favoured solution for V/STOL projects of 1958-69. Rolls-Royce, far more than any other company, developed very small and light lift jets (HBPR fans for civil airline applications) which could be installed in large numbers for use only during the takeoff and landing phases of each mission. Tailoring the lift jets and vectored main engine(s) exactly to the mission could lead to a very competitive aircraft. The fastest V/STOL in history (Mirage III-V, Mach 2·04 in 1966) and Soviet Yak-36MP (Forger) both use separate lift jets, but interest today is at a low ebb. The GD Convair Model 218V typifies V/STOL studies of the 1970s using separate lift jets, in this case for an agile Navy fighter with one vectored main engine and the lift jets between the inlet ducts.

Pivoted engines

Superficially this may seem the most attractive of all V/STOL schemes, because the engines are quite uncompromised and give perfect efficiency in the conventional-flight mode, and nothing has to be added to the aircraft but hinges. Indeed, one of the most recent tilt-nacelle projects, the British Aerospace P.103, uses the two widely separated engines with simple nozzle deflectors to control the aircraft in hovering or transition flight. This eliminates the need for an RCS (reaction control system) fed by engine bleed air, which in turn allows the engines to give full thrust without the loss due to RCS bleed. One of the drawbacks of the tilting nacelle aircraft is that it is difficult to get the thrust near the aircraft centreline, though of course it can be done with twin tail booms. With engines mounted well outboard, as in the P.103, loss of one engine causes immediate and unrecoverable roll.

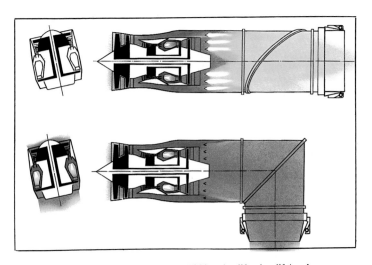

Above: Though popular in the early 1960s, the lift-plus-lift/cruise formula is now recognised as not competitive. This is despite the fact that specialized lift jets (engine at left) can be made amazingly small and light for any given thrust. Remaining studies usually involve only two or three lift jets to add lift to an aircraft whose vectored main engine is sized for the cruise thrust requirement and does not have the power to lift the aircraft alone.

Below: The tilting-engine or pivoted-nacelle arrangement leaves the main engines perfectly suited to cruise propulsion and the only extras, apart from the hinges and flexible pipes and cables, are a simple nozzle giving limited jet vectoring, and a control link. The main engines in a twin-engined fighter can even provide hovering control and trim, but engine failure is serious.

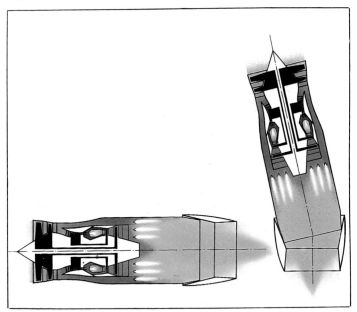

Tupolev Blackjack

Origin: The OKB of Andrei N. Tupolev, Soviet Union.
Type: Strategic bomber and missile carrier.
Engines: Four large augmented turbofans or turbojets (possibly of Koliesov type) each in the 48,500lb (22000kg) thrust class.
Dimensions: (estimated) Span (spread, 20° sweep) 177ft (54m), (max sweep, 57°) 135ft (41·2m); length 171ft (52·1m); height 47ft 6in (14·5m); wing area 4,000sq ft (370m²).
Weights: (estimated) Empty 275,600lb (125000kg); internal fuel 368,000lb (167000kg); max 683,400lb (310000kg).
Performance: (estimated) Max speed (hi, clean) 1,200kt (1,382mph, 2224km/h, Mach 2·1); max combat radius with full weapon load 4,536 miles (7300km); endurance 14h.
Armament: Unknown, but includes an estimated bombload of at least 36,000lb (16330kg) in a large internal bay, or alternatively several externally carried cruise missiles including the so-called AS-X-15, the large new weapon carried by current-production Bears.
History: First observed by West 25 November 1981; IOC (DoD estimate) 1987.
User: Soviet Union.

Though it is not certain that it is a product of the Tupolev OKB, the giant swing-wing bomber called Blackjack by NATO is so big and of such a character that no other design bureau seems possible. It was first seen on a satellite reconnaissance film on the date given above. A prototype was parked near Tu-144 SSTs, enabling comparative assessment to be made.

The latest figures are given above, most of them coming from the DoD. The previous estimate of span at max sweep was only 95ft (29m) and max weight a mere 575,000lb (260800kg), whereas the length has been revised down from 180ft (55m). There now seems little doubt that the configuration is almost precisely the same as that of the USAF B-1, though the Tupolev bomber is much larger. According to estimates it is also faster, though probably this is less important than its defensive electronic systems, "stealth" qualities and ability to follow terrain in all weathers at high speed.

Certainly Blackjack has nothing whatever in common with the much smaller Tu-22M, and it may not even come from the Tupolev OKB (though it is hard to

Below: The first glimpse of Blackjack to be published in the West was this readout from a reconnaissance sensor showing a prototype of the new bomber parked near Tu-144 SSTs, one of which is seen in the rear. The location was Ramenskoye test centre.

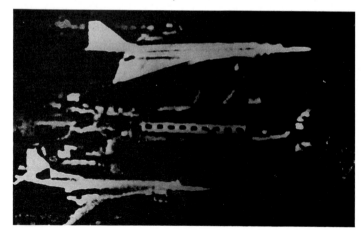

imagine any other source). The giant fixed wing glove, which extends almost to the nose, and the two pairs of engines mounted underneath its rear portion, have much in common with the Tu-144D SST, though it is extremely unlikely that the similarity is more than superficial.

Instead of cruising at Mach 2-plus at extreme altitude the bomber will spend almost all of each mission at subsonic speed just above the Earth's surface. It has been surmised that its weapons are carried in a box between the engine group on each side. With or without flight refuelling this aircraft clearly has the ability to reach virtually any target on Earth from Soviet or client-state bases, and its nature (unlike the Tu-22M) is deeply strategic. Thus it is unlikely to bother with anti-ship missiles, but it is expected to carry the AS-X-15 cruise weapon in multiple installations.

The gigantic new production factory being swiftly completed next to the existing Tupolev plant at Kazan is seen as the source of the production machines, which are predicted to become operational in 1987. Initially they are expected to replace M-4 Bison and Tu-95 Bear-A.

Below: A US DoD impression of Tupolev Blackjack strategic bombers operating in the cruise regime with wings swept back at high altitude — probably an unlikely combination. This is certainly the heaviest combat aircraft every built.

ACAP

Origin: Bell Helicopter Textron and Sikorsky Aircraft, USA.
Type: Research helicopters with composite airframe.
Engines: Two turboshafts, (Bell D292) two 650hp Avco Lycoming LTS101-650C, (Sikorsky S-75) two 650hp Allison 250-C30. Remaining data for S-75;
Dimensions: Diameter of main rotor 44ft 0in (13·41m); length of fuselage 43ft 6in (13·26m); height overall 14ft 9in (4·5m).
Weights: Empty 5,944lb (2696kg); max 8,470lb (3842kg).
Performance: Max speed 174mph (280km/h); mission endurance 2·3h.
History: Contract award April 1981, first flight (both) late 1984.
User: USA (Army).

The Advanced Composite Airframe Program is intended to provide knowledge useful in future production of V/STOL aircraft, such as the LHX described later. Goals include: 22 per cent reduction in weight, 17 per cent saving in cost, survivability in a crash at 42ft (12·8m)/s vertical descent, and reduced radar signature. Attention is addressed to the airframe structure only, though in due course the dynamic parts (rotors, hubs, transmission and gearboxes) may also come in for attention. Two companies won the major awards, the design and supporting tests being completed in 1981-82, followed by construction of three airframes — a Tool Proof Article, Static Test Article and Flight Test Vehicle — in 1983-84. The two FTVs, which are complete flying helicopters, will be due to fly at about the time this book appears.

Both are based on existing machines, the Bell 222 and Sikorsky S-76, though similarity is really confined to the engines and dynamic parts. The airframe structures are totally new, made of GRP, Kevlar, graphite (CFRP) and other composites. Bell's ACAP, the D292, incorporates roof, floors and fuel-cell bulkheads by Grumman Aerospace, a particularly experienced composites

Below: In the D292 Bell Helicopter Textron has adhered to a tailwheel type landing gear; other Bells use skids or (Model 222) retractable nosewheel-type gear. In fact the 222 was the starting point, the landing gear being a major visual difference.

manufacturer, and landing gears by Menasco. In each case the landing gears are non-retractable. The D292 is designed to carry a flight crew of two and two passengers, but Sikorsky's S-75 has been configured for six passengers. The S-75 incorporates a lower tub section (the bottom half of the main fuselage) by LTV and a complete tailcone and tail by Hercules (producer of large composite rocket motor cases).

At present ACAP is regarded as a pure research programme, and neither helicopter meets the requirements of the broad and far-ranging LHX programme. On the other hand, while the enhanced capability in composite airframes will be of great advantage in the LHX programme, and give Bell and Sikorsky a big competitive edge, it is not beyond the bounds of possibility that either or both machines might later replace the conventional metal 222 and S-76.

Sikorsky has also designed and built two composite rear fuselages for the bigger H-60, under USAF contract. The original structure had 856 detail parts, 75 assemblies and 13,600 fasteners, while the composite figures are 104, 10 and 1,700. Cost reduction is 38 per cent.

Above: Sikorsky's S-75 differs from the S-76 in almost every part, except for the engines, transmission and rotors. One should not draw too many conclusions from the fact that empty weight exceeds that of an S-76 while maximum weight will be much less.

Agusta A129 Mangusta

Origin: Costruzioni Aeronautiche Giovanni Agusta SpA, Italy.
Type: Anti-armour and scout helicopter.
Engines: Two 1,035hp Rolls-Royce Gem 2 Mk 1004D turboshaft engines.
Dimensions: Diameter of four-blade main rotor 39ft 0·5in (11·9m); length of fuselage 40ft 3·27in (12·275m); height overall 10ft 11·9in (3·35m); main rotor disc area 1,197sq ft (111·2m²).
Weights: Empty (equipped) 5,575lb (2529kg); max 8,157lb (3700kg).
Performance: Max speed (SL at 8,080lb, 3600kg) 168mph (270km/h); cruising speed 155mph (250km/h); hovering ceiling 7,850ft (2390m); endurance (anti-tank, no reserve) 2h 30min.
Armament: Four weapon attachments, inners 661lb (300kg) rating, outers 441lb (200kg), all able to tilt +3°/−12° from horizontal. Outers will normally carry two quad launchers of TOW missiles, with the option of HOT or Hellfire as alternative; various gun pods can be carried, or up to 52 rockets of 70mm size in four launchers.
History: First flight 15 September 1983; operational deployment due in early 1986.
User: Expected to be Italy, followed by other countries.

One of the strange features of NATO procurement is that France and West Germany were in 1984 ponderously setting forth on the development of a dedicated anti-tank helicopter for service after 1991 while in Italy an exactly similar machine is already flying! The A129 is Western Europe's only helicopter in this class, and it has been planned to meet the needs of all customers until at least the year 2000. At first it was hoped to use 450hp Allison engines, but increased mission demands led to the present engines of over twice the power. Later it is even possible that further growth may require Gem engines of around 1,500hp or alternatively the 1,700hp T700 engine used in the AH-64 Apache.

Right: Among the weapons currently being qualified for use on the A129 are the quad mountings of Hughes TOW anti-tank missiles as already used by the A109A. Other ordnance includes 12·7-mm gun pods, rocket launchers and Hellfire laser missiles.

Below: The first of the four A129 prototypes on a test flight. By mid-1984 the flight programme had gone very well indeed, and Agusta was feeling confident not only of the 1986 in-service date, but also of a growing number of export orders.

Today's A129 is a refined machine which from the start has naturally been planned for maximum effectiveness and lethality on the battlefield, with the greatest possible protection and resistance to hostile gunfire up to 23mm. Almost the only surprising feature is location of the TOW telescopic sight, with laser and FLIR, very low in the nose where the entire machine must be exposed in order to see the enemy. Agusta has worked with Martin Marietta on an MMS (mast-mounted sight) and this may later replace the nose location.

No requirement exists for a chin turret or other trainable guns, but the Italian army has called for a comprehensive EW installation including radar and laser warning receivers, IR jammer and chaff/flare dispenser. Equipment includes a PNVS as on the Apache, integrated helmet sight system, and — for the first time in a helicopter — an IMS (integrated multiplex system) to centralize management of all subsystems.

The Italian army expects to receive six A129s for training and either 60 or 90 for use in 30-aircraft squadrons.

Bell AHIP, OH-58D

Origin: Bell Helicopter Textron, USA.
Type: Near-term scout helicopter.
Engine: One 650hp Allison 250-C30 turboshaft.
Dimensions: Diameter of main rotor 35ft 0in (10·67m); length of fuselage 33ft 10in (10·31m); height overall 12ft 9·5in (3·9m).
Weights: Empty 2,825lb (1281kg); max 4,500lb (2041kg).
Performance: Max speed 147mph (237km/h); cruising speed 127mph (204km/h); range (max fuel, no reserves) 345 miles (556km).
Armament: Two MLMS (multipurpose lightweight missile system) missiles.
History: First flight September 1983; completion of qualification testing June 1984.
User: USA (Army).

To meet the Army's need for a "near-term scout", to fly missions until the appropriate version of LHX becomes available, an AHIP (Army Helicopter Improvement Program) was organised, which Bell won in September 1981. Five OH-58A Kiowa helicopters from the Army inventory have been completely updated to the standard planned for the OH-58D, which meets the need for an interim reconnaissance aircraft for use over the battlefield, able to fly surveillance and intelligence-gathering missions as well as supporting attack helicopter missions and directing artillery fire. Under a $151 million contract the five modified Kiowas have an MMS (mast-mounted sight) with laser/FLIR/TV, completely new Sperry cockpits with digital multiplex data highways and integrated programmable displays, advanced EW threat warning, an airborne target handoff system, and comprehensive all-weather avionics including doppler, strapdown INS and night-vision goggles.

The MLMS missile is the air-launched version of Stinger, an infantry anti-aircraft SAM. It will probably be carried in a two-round box on the right side, and guidance will be at two wavelengths in the IR and UV (ultraviolet) regions. It would not be effective against hostile armour, which is not a required mission, but against hostile aircraft and possibly various soft surface targets. Other weapons might be added, but already the max weight is 50 per cent up on that of the OH-58A.

In due course it is expected that Bell will receive contracts totalling at least $2,000 million to bring at least 578 OH-58As up to OH-58D standard. This would take until 1991.

Below: By mid-1984 the definitive standard of the OH-58D had been agreed, the five prototypes (of which this is one) having been flown intensively to prove the equipment and systems. The 578 planned helicopters will bridge the gap until an LHX arrives.

Bell AH-1T+ SuperCobra

Origin: Bell Helicopter Textron, USA.
Type: Attack helicopter.
Engines: Two 1,625hp General Electric T700-GE-401 turboshafts.
Dimensions: Diameter of main rotor 48ft 0in (14·63m); length of fuselage 48ft 2in (14·68m); height overall 14ft 2in (4·32m).
Weights: Empty about 8,300lb (3765kg); max, over 14,000lb (6350kg).
Performance: Max speed 193mph (311km/h); cruising speed 184mph (296km/h).
Armament: Chin turret with M197 gun and 750 rounds of 20mm, choice of eight TOW or eight Hellfire anti-armour guided missiles, range of 2·75in or 5in (70 or 127mm) rockets or various dropped stores.
History: First flight (AH-1) 7 September 1965, (AH-1T with T700 engines) April 1980, (AH-1T+) 16 November 1983.
User: USA (Marine Corps).

Famed as the world's first dedicated "gunship" armed helicopter, the AH-1 HueyCobra has been developed through many variations. Most of these have revolved around armament fit, avionics and such features as changing from a rounded to a flat-plate cockpit canopy, but in parallel with these has been a progressive increase in installed horsepower. The original mass-produced version, the AH-1, had a T53 engine flat-rated at 1,100hp, and this is also used in the AH-1G. The main versions now in use have a total of 1,800hp, the AH-1S family having a greatly uprated T53 engine and the AH-1J SeaCobra having a T400 engine with this power only theoretically available (900hp from each power section), the transmission still being limited to 1,100hp continuous rating but the T400 giving an element of engine-out safety. The latest version in service is the AH-1T Improved SeaCobra, of the US Marine Corps, an entirely new transmission being able to transmit the full power of a 2,050hp T400-WV-402 coupled engine unit.

Even this is nowhere near the limit, and in 1980 Bell successfully tested an AH-1T powered by two quite separate T700 engines of the type fitted to the UH-60A Black Hawk. This gave a tremendous increase in performance at heavier weights, especially in the most adverse "hot and high" conditions. After full evaluation by Navy and Marine test pilots — including DCoS (Air) Lt-Gen Tom Miller, the "father of the US Harrier" — the Marines obtained Congressional approval for a production run of 44 AH-1T+ SuperCobras, the most versatile and capable armed helicopter yet, it is claimed. The designation, sometimes written AH-1TPlus, may be changed. Batches of 22 SuperCobras are expected to be funded in Fiscal 1985 and 1986, for use in the anti-armour, troop helicopter escort, multi-weapon fire support, recon by fire, and search/target acquisition roles.

Below: Essentially the same size as the first Cobra of 1965, the Super is three times as powerful, and much more deadly.

Boeing Vertol Research

In 1971 the US Department of Defense initiated the development of an HLH (heavy-lift helicopter) research programme to provide knowledge in such areas as an 8,000hp advanced turboshaft engine (Allison T701), 18,000hp transmission system and gearboxes, FBW flight control system, 92ft (28m) rotor with fail-safe glassfibre blades, and 35t cargo handling system with dual tandem hoists. In 1973 the project expanded to include the complete XCH-62 helicopter, shown in the artist's impression, but in 1975 work had to cease because of lack of programme funds. This was clearly a long-term error, because $180 million had been spent, the first flight prototype was virtually complete, and only $26 million was needed.'

Since 1980 Boeing Vertol has received three contracts to develop and test the final elements in the transmission, including crucial spiral-bevel and planetary gears, all operating at torque levels twice anything attempted outside the Soviet Union. The XCH-62 has never ceased to remain a viable and needed helicopter, which would fill an obvious major gap in the defence capability of all Western air forces. In 1984 Boeing Vertol was still testing the XCH-62 aft and combiner gearboxes, fully validating the recent design changes and clearing the way for production should this ever get into the DoD budget. The stored aircraft could still fly in 1986.

In another programme the company has spent its own funds building the Model 360, a helicopter similar in size and configuration to the CH-46 Sea Knight but with the airframe and rotors (including blades and also the hubs) constructed almost entirely of advanced lightweight composites. Typical of the advanced features of the 360 is an FBL (fly-by-light) secondary flight-control system with fibre optics. It should have flown before this book appears.

Below: This impression of an HLH lifting an M110 SP howitzer could have been real by 1975 had any major attempt been made to deploy this helicopter. As it is, a decade has been lost, and because of inflation the final cost will be multiplied by about four, but an eventual CH-62 (if it ever happens) will be rather better than the helicopter of the 1970s would have been.

EH Industries EH.101

Origin: EH Industries Ltd., 50/50 Agusta (Italy) and Westland (UK).
Type: Multirole helicopters with variants for naval ASW, SAR, utility and passenger transport.
Engines: Three 1,729shp General Electric T700-401 turboshafts, with option of later fitting three 2,100shp Rolls-Royce Turboméca RTM 322-01.
Dimensions: Diameter of five-blade main rotor 61ft 0in (18·59m); length (overall, rotors turning) 75ft 1·6in (22·9m); (rotor and tail folded) 52ft 0in (15·85m); height (overall, rotors turning) 21ft 4in (6·5m); main-rotor disc area 2,924·8sq ft (271·72m²).
Weights: Empty (naval) 15,500lb (7031kg); max (naval) 28,660lb (13000kg), (utility/passenger) 31,504lb (14290kg).
Performance: Max cruising speed (naval) 173mph (278km/h), (utility) 184mph (296km/h), range (transport, 30 passengers) 633 miles (1020km), (ferry) 1,150 miles (1850km); endurance on station (naval, ASW dunking with full weapon load) 5h.
Armament: (Naval) Four AS torpedoes or wide range of other stores including anti-ship missiles.
History: First flight, due mid-1986; service entry (naval) 1990.
Users: Not yet ordered.

By far the most expensive helicopter ever produced in Western Europe, the EH.101 is a joint 50/50 programme by companies in Britain and Italy, with each partner handling design and manufacture of its own assigned portions. It should have a bright future, because though it was initially planned as an SKR (Sea King replacement) it has already found other roles including that of commercial passenger airliner. It will easily outperform the Sea King, not least because of its much higher installed power, yet in some ways it is actually more compact. In 1984 the design of this initial naval EH.101 had been finalised, and construction of five prototypes has been authorised.

The naval type has the highest priority, but because of its reduced complexity the commercial 30-seater is expected to enter service first, in 1989. The proposed military utility model, with an aft ramp door and disposable load of ▶

Below: The first provisional three-view of the basic military version of EH.101 published in May 1981. Since then the design has altered considerably, and in general the helicopters now in detail engineering and prototype construction are better-looking.

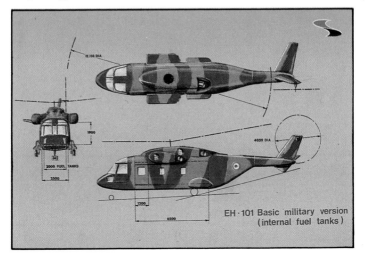

EH·101 Basic military version (internal fuel tanks)

▶ 14,769lb (6699kg), could have the same timing. This model would airlift 28 equipped troops, or 24 troops and full equipment and supporting stores, over a radius of 230 miles (370km).

The naval EH.101 will be packed with avionics for all-weather navigation and automatic flight in all ASW, ship-landing, surveillance and similar roles. A large radar will be mounted under the forward fuselage, the latter being watertight but not having a boat hull as in the Sea King. Fairey single-wheel main gears retract backwards into the sponsons in all versions.

Operation is to be possible from a small frigate in Sea State 6, with the wind gusting from any heading at speeds up to 57mph (93km/h). One of the required capabilities is to pass OTH (over the horizon) target data to a friendly surface ship and guide the latter's missiles to the distant target. Equipment will include the helicopter's own ASW or ASV missiles, as well as (for example) small arms for use to arrest smugglers.

Full launch aid for the project, an initial £120 million, was voted by the two participating governments in early 1984. The Royal and Italian navies are stated to have requirements for 50 and 38 EH.101s, respectively, the former having announced the type as standard equipment on the Type 23 frigates. Rolls-Royce has always wished to provide propulsion, but for reasons of timing the GE engine was selected at least for the prototypes.

Below: A model of the basic ASW version of EH.101 in Royal Navy colours. This is the variant on which maximum effort is being applied, though, because it is simpler, the airline version is expected to enter service first, probably in 1989.

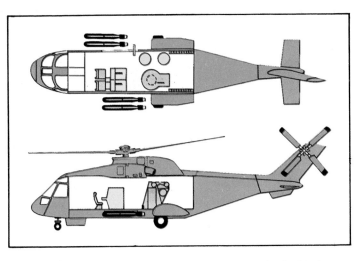

Above: The ASW model will have two operator consoles (yellow), a large dunking sonar (light green) and racks for sonobouys aft (with two tube dispensers, dark yellow), a rescue hoist by the door and up to four torpedoes. It can operate autonomously using any kind of sonar system.

Hughes NOTAR

Origin: Hughes Helicopters, USA.
Type: Helicopter with no tail rotor.
Engine: (OH-6A) One 317hp Allison T63-A-5A turboshaft.
Dimensions: Diameter of main rotor 26ft 4·8in (8·05m); length of fuselage 25ft 6in (7·8m); height overall 8ft 8·5in (2·7m).
Weights: Empty about 1,000lb (454kg); max about 2,500lb (1134kg).
Performance: Max speed, has exceeded 140mph (225km/h) in testing; production machines would be much faster.
Armament: Depends on mission.
History: First flight (OH-6A) 27 February 1963, (OH-6A NOTAR) 17 December 1981.
User: Planned for USA (Army) and civil applications.

Now a subsidiary of McDonnell Douglas, Hughes Helicopters has more than 5,000 helicopters currently in worldwide operation, all of the classic configuration with an anti-torque and yaw-control tail rotor. In May 1981 the company announced a contract from DARPA and the US Army for flight testing a NOTAR (no tail rotor) helicopter to validate and refine the company's idea for countering main-rotor torque by means of side-thrust on an enlarged tail boom. This thrust is generated by aerodynamic circulation induced by ejection of a high-velocity jet from a thin slit along the underside of the left side of the boom, with yaw control from a rotating 90° angled nozzle at the extreme tail. Air supply to the slit and nozzle is from an auxiliary engine-driven fan. The test programme was continuing in 1984, the vehicle being a modified OH-6A. Overall efficiency is similar to that of a tail rotor, but without the noise and vulnerability. This would be especially useful in "nap of the Earth" combat missions.

Hughes has devoted great attention to reducing helicopter noise, and following "The Quiet One", a special research version of the Model 500M, work is in hand on a Higher Harmonic Control test programme which reduces noise and vibration.

Below: The tail-rotor-equipped Higher Harmonic Control OH-6 has a computer-controlled vibration suppression system developed with the US Army and NASA. It is seen as crucial to accurate weapon and avionic performance by the AH-64A (background) and LHX.

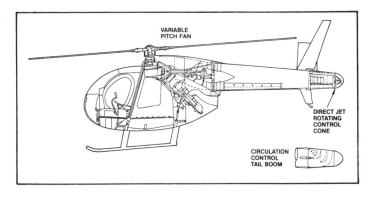

Above: This drawing shows the geometry of the NOTAR OH-6A but not the full-length slit along the lower left side of the fat tail boom. The sheet of high-speed air blown from this slit generates the side force, replacing the normal tail rotor.

Below: Testing a Notar helicopter inside a protective whirl stand at Hughes' Culver City plant in 1984, during tests to see how the main rotor downwash affects the airflow round the boom.

LHX

Origin: Contractor yet to be selected in USA.
Type: Two versions for scout/attack and utility helicopter missions.
Engine(s): Various single or twin turboshaft engines.
Dimensions: Typically "small helicopter" size.
Weights: Loaded, typically from 6,000lb (2722kg) to 10,000lb (4500kg).
Performance: Max speed may be specified as high as 345mph (555km/h);
mission radius depends on mission and LHX/U or LHX/SCAT variations.
Armament: (LHX/U) none, or possibly a self-protection missile; (LHX/SCAT)
range of existing weapons including a gun of 20mm or greater calibre, Hellfire
missiles, MLMS (air-launched Stinger) and other ordnance.
History: ARTI phase (see text) expected to last until 1987; FSED planned for
1988-1991 (first flight about 1988), with production from 1992 for IOC in 1995.
User: USA (Army initially).

**Below: Artist's concept of how a Bell Helicopter Textron tilt-rotor LHX
might look in the anti-armour role. LHX is potentially a gigantic
programme, and the US Army is trying to keep an open mind and see
which proposals for the various tasks look most promising.**

At rare intervals the US armed forces come up with a mixture of requirements which, being met by variations on the same basic type, can generate a market so large as to support the development of a whole new generation of technology. In early 1983 the LHX (light helicopter experimental) programme had only dimly been discerned. Today every major helicopter manufacturer in the USA is exhorting its technical staff "This is a programme we simply must win". In fact the answer may not be a helicopter at all, but a tilt-rotor or (most unlikely in view of political difficulties) a vectored-thrust jet. Moreover, there are three main missions and groups of existing helicopters to be replaced, and two distinct versions of LHX are envisaged to meet the requirements.

LHX-U or LHX/U is the utility model. This will be basically a front-line transport to replace the UH-1 Iroquois (Huey) in all utility versions, the US Army requirement in this role being about 2,000 aircraft. Smaller than the UH-60A Black Hawk, LHX/U will carry a squad of six to eight troops, and could also carry EW loads (Elint/Comint/jammers and the like), cargo slung internally or externally, or fly casevac missions with stretcher patients.

LHX-SCAT (LHX/SCAT) is the scout/attack model. This would replace the AH-1 Cobra and UH-1M in gunship roles, about 1,100 being needed for this purpose, and the OH-6A and OH-58C in the scout role, the number in this case fluctuating between 900 and 1,800. Thus the total buy for the US Army alone is likely to be not less than 4,000 and probably more. ▶

▶ The whole programme is looming so large that it is being underpinned by major research programmes, notably ARTI (Advanced Rotorcraft Technology Integration) for the airframe and systems, and ATDE (Advanced Technology Demonstrator Engine) for propulsion. The two ATDE finalists in 1984 were Allison with its 800-1,000hp Model 280 (previously designated GMA 500) and Avco Lycoming with its 1,200hp PLT34. Predictably, power requirements keep rising, and by mid-1984 it was clear that an engine of over 1,000hp would be needed.

ARTI is funding specific research, and other major efforts will also bear directly upon LHX technology. Extensive use of advanced composite structures will be needed to create a V/STOL aircraft of unprecedented compactness, high strength and light weight. The demand for comprehensive all-weather navigation, NOE (nap of the Earth) flight at night or in fog, advanced EW systems and fire-control and target acquisition for various weapons will make LHX perhaps the most advanced V/STOL from the avionics viewpoint ever attempted. To meet the demands in extremely limited space/weight specifications VHSIC (very high-speed integrated circuit) technology will be used throughout, together with FBL (fly by light) optical-fibre flight control and data highways. It is hoped to have a one-man cockpit, and the SCAT version could well be a single-seater.

Bell Helicopter
Because of its knowledge from the XV-15 and JVX programme Bell is uniquely able to propose an agile tilt-rotor LHX, the final report on which was delivered in 1983. Bell is also contracted to submit further proposals using conventional

helicopter designs. The BAT (Bell Advanced Tilt-rotor) is the SCAT submission offering a speed of 350mph (563km/h) and ferry range of 2,415 miles (3887km); it has a single ejection seat, retractable gear and weapons concealed internally. The same wing/engine/rotor would fit the big-bodied LHX/U version.

Boeing Vertol

This company has teamed with Boeing Military Airplane Co for avionic system integration, Westinghouse for sensors and Harris Corporation for rotorcraft ►

Above: Mock-up of the BAT (Bell Advanced Tilt-rotor), likely to be a major candidate for the LHX SCAT mission. Span across the 20ft 6in (6·25m) rotors is the same as the diameter of the rotor of an AH-1S Modernized Cobra helicopter. Bell claims a lift/drag ratio "50 per cent better than potential high-performance helicopters" and the impressive speed and range given in the text above. Beautifully streamlined, BAT would expose its internal weapons only at the last moment. The company claims BAT is cost effective.

Left: Boeing Vertol artwork showing one of the company's ideas for an LHX operating in the SCAT mission. To shield the pilot from possible laser blinding, his view of the world is synthesistic, ie, generated entirely by sensors. Radiating waves show the range and direction of ground targets being determined by the mast-mounted multisensor sight, while a missile is fired at one target and the gun at another. Like all LHX candidates this helicopter is highly streamlined and should have a low radar or IR signature. Vulnerability remains a problem.

Above: A slightly fanciful LHX/SCAT proposed by Hughes, naturally with NOTAR but also fitted with a swept wing. This suggestion of the supersonic jet fighter shows Hughes is on the right wavelength with SCAT, but a new form of main lifting rotor would be needed.

Above right: To help it win in the LHX programme Sikorsky will fly this Shadow (rebuilt S-76) soon after this book appears. The new single-place cockpit in the nose will prove literally instrumental in defining pilot workloads and interfaces, with the support of Bendix, Kaiser, Litton, Collins, Singer and others.

▶ systems automation and pilot displays. Boeing Vertol is well advanced with two ARTI programmes: ICC (integrated cockpit configuration) and Adocs (advanced digital optical control system); Westinghouse is including advanced radars (probably conformal) in its sensors, and Harris is helping integrate the complex avionics systems. An accompanying artist's impression shows a single-main-rotor helicopter (if it has a tail rotor, it is hard to see how it misses the main blades) busy with mast-mounted sensors, trainable gun and missiles.

Hughes Helicopters
Chairman of the company board Robert C. Little recently stressed the McDonnell Douglas ownership view the LHX "as a must-win program. The competition should be shaking in their boots. We have the resources to knock them off-balance". Virtually the entire Hughes R&D effort is focussed on LHX, and the company is teamed with Hughes Aircraft (subsystems integrator) and Honeywell (overall systems integrator). The artist's impression shows one of the fighter-like NOTAR (see separate description) LHX/SCAT proposals, though it is doubtful that swept wings and leading-edge root strakes would really be features of such a vehicle. The Hughes team have studied energy absorption of various retracting landing gears, integrated cockpits and the prospects for using a modifed AH-64 Apache as an ARTI research/demo vehicle.

Sikorsky
Nobody is going out harder to win LHX than this division of United Technologies, which has teamed with sister-divisions HamStan and Norden Systems, and also with Martin Marietta, Northrop and Rockwell Collins. HamStan is handling flight control and voice warning and command systems (see introduction section, Cockpits); Norden is involved with C³I and VHSIC, Martin with sensors and weapon control, Northrop with FLIR and advanced concepts in target acquisition and designation, while Rockwell is handling

system architectures, displays and com/nav avionics. Artist's impressions show the ARTI Shadow (Sikorsky helicopter advanced demonstrator of operator workload) which is an ARTI cockpit mounted on an S-76, due to fly in late 1984. Another shows an LHX with rear thruster and ABC type rotor (see Sikorsky X-59 ABC entry on pages 156 and 157).

Mil Mi-28 (Havoc)

Origin: The OKB named for Mikhail L. Mil, Soviet Union.
Type: Armed attack helicopter.
Engines: Probably two 2,330shp Isotov TV3-117 series turboshafts.
Dimensions: Diameter of main rotor, probably about 55ft 9in (17m); size generally similar to Mi-24.
Weights: Empty probably about 13,230lb (6000kg); max about 22,046lb (10000kg).
Performance: Max speed, in excess of 200mph (322km/h); cruising speed in action 186mph (300km/h); mission radius (lo throughout) 150 miles (240km).
Armament: Not yet known, but clearly heavy and varied.
History: First flight, prior to 1982; service entry expected 1984-5.
Users: Soviet Union.

The Soviet Union and its client states, including Afghanistan, operate thousands of Mi-24 ("Hind") helicopters which combine various formidable weapon and sensor capabilities with a cabin for (typically) eight armed troops. Not surprisingly the same, or a closely similar, engine/rotor system has now appeared on a dedicated armed gunship type helicopter with no cabin, but just a tandem cockpit for a crew of two. Little is yet known about it in the West, beyond a crude side-view drawing published in the DoD 1984 edition of *Soviet Military Power* which appears to be based on the US Army Hughes AH-64 Apache. The Mi-28, whose designation is given apparently with assurance, is said to be "very agile". Its gross weight is estimated above to be rather less than that of the Mi-24, though it probably carries a heavy mass of armour as well as an extremely comprehensive kit of sensors and protective EW/ECM systems. A small detail is that the DoD artist indicated the tail rotor on the right side, whereas all recent Mil helicopters of this family have it on the left.

MBB/Aérospatiale PAH-2/HAC

Origin: MBB, West Germany; Aérospatiale, France.
Type: Anti-tank helicopter.
Engines: (proposed) Two MTU/Turboméca MTM 385 turboshafts, each to be rated in the 800shp class.
Dimensions: Not decided, but the four-blade main rotor would have a diameter of about 42ft (12·8m).
Weights: Max, about 9,260lb (4200kg).
Performance: Max speed about 155mph (250km/h).
Armament: Primary armament would comprise eight Euromissile HOT missiles; West German PAH-2s would also carry four Stinger (MLMS) self-defence AAMs.
History: First flight, possibly 1987.
Users: France, Germany.

After an extremely uncertain and protracted early history, in which at least two years have been lost through indecision, this dedicated anti-tank helicopter at last went ahead as a joint 50/50 programme sponsored by the governments of France and West Germany in November 1983. Not until 28 May 1984 was there any news of a bilateral agreement and a Memorandum of Understanding covering the development phase.

The basic concept is that of a tandem-seat machine with fixed tailwheel landing gear, main rotor with four GRP blades, stub wings carrying the weapons, a stabilized nose-mounted sight, and comprehensive all-weather and night avionics. What makes the programme all the stranger is that it is in all respects an exact reinvention of the Italian A129, which is already flying and has mature engines.

Should the PAH-2/HAC actually go ahead it is hoped to deliver production examples from 1992. The difference in timing and the need to develop a special engine means that, on the most optmistic estimate, the unit price will be 50 per cent higher than that of the existing A129.

It is planned that there should be three distinct versions. The best-known designation, PAH-2, is actually a purely German model of which 200 are needed from 1992. It will have a nose-mounted sight for pilot and gunner. HAP (Hélicoptère d'Appui Protection) is the initial French version, with a new 30mm

Below: General-arrangement of the HAP French attack/escort version, whose massive 30mm nose gun has to be balanced by rearwards shift of the sponsons carrying the other weapons. This much-delayed helicopter family risks losing the immediate market to the existing A129, and the future 1990s market to the much more advanced US choice of LHX/SCAT.

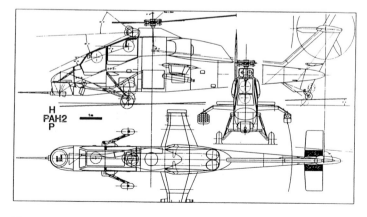

GIAT cannon and AATCP (Mistral) close-range AAMs. In 1995 the French will also need HAC 3G (Hélicoptère Anti-Char 3rd generation), with PARS.3 missiles (to be developed by EMDG and also to be retrofitted to PAH-2) and a mast-mounted sight. The French need 200 machines in all, about 100 of each version.

Above: A model of the basic German PAH-2, displayed by MBB. The various delays have not been wasted as the design has been refined and improved, but it is difficult to see what it can offer that is not already available in the A129.

Below: General arrangement of the HAC 3G anti-tank version, which the French expect to put into service in about 1995. This restores the long-span French weapon sponsons to the normal position in line with the rotor, adds a mast-mounted sight and replaces the gun with a pilot night-vision system.

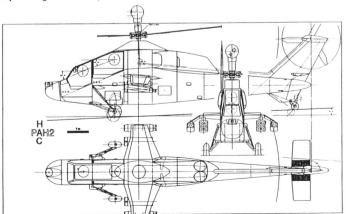

Sikorsky S-69 (XH-59A) ABC

Origin: Sikorsky Aircraft, USA.

Type: Experimental-rotor research demonstrator.

Engines: One 1,825hp Pratt & Whitney Canada PT6T-3 coupled twin turboshaft and two 3,000lb (1361kg) thrust Pratt & Whitney J60-3A turbojets.

Dimensions: Diameter of three-blade main rotors 36ft 0in (10·97m); length of fuselage 40ft 9in (overall 41ft 5in, 12·62m); height overall 12ft 11in (3·94m).

Weights: Gross (helicopter) 9,000lb (4082kg), (plus jets) 11,100lb (5035kg).

Performance: Maximum speed (level) 276 mph (445km/h), (in 7° dive) 303mph (487km/h); ceiling 25,500ft (7770m); rate of climb 5,000ft (1524m)/min; acceleration from rest to 213mph (353km/h) in 28s.

History: First flight July 1973, (with auxiliary jets) early 1978 (date not announced).

User: USA.

One of the most successful research helicopter programmes, the ABC (Advancing Blade Concept) uses two counter-rotating rotors each with three stiff hingeless blades, no tail rotor being needed. At high speeds the lift is supplied by advancing blades on each side; the retreating blades are almost unloaded, so the usual problem of retreating blade stall is avoided. Among the advantages are: higher top speed than a conventional helicopter, full manoeuvrability up to maximum speed, reduced noise, good hover efficiency and, with auxiliary (jet) propulsion, very high acceleration with the fuselage essentially level. The initial tests were funded by the Army and Sikorsky, but the high-speed programme has both Army and Navy funds. Prolonged testing at Fort Rucker led to the Army stating that the ABC has "excellent potential for application to tactical Army aircraft".

Sikorsky has done much work on a proposed XH-59B with twin T700 engines (about 1,700hp each) driving a new rotor with hingeless composite blades and a ducted propeller at the tail. (A very similar machine is mentioned in the LHX entry on an earlier page.) This had not entered the hardware stage in mid-1984, but there seems little doubt that Sikorsky will eventually win a major contract for an LHX candidate with ABC principles. Sikorsky claims the concept offers unrivalled performance and operational advantages for an attack helicopter, a SEMA (Special Electronic Missions Aircraft) and a future SAR machine. All would fly at 260mph (418km/h), carry a payload of about 4,400lb (2000kg), have a one-engine ceiling out of ground effect on a 35° (95°F) day of 4,000ft (1219m) and have very impressive range and endurance, such as an SAR mission to a radius of 288 miles (463km), 20min hover and return with six rescuees, whilst burdened by 2,360lb (1070kg) of mission equipment.

Below: The first XH-59A fitted with its J60 booster turbojets, seen with landing gear extended. It is the only helicopter to have exceeded 300mph (186km/h) without wings.

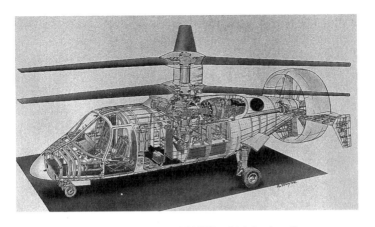

Above: Cutaway of the proposed XH-59B, which is virtually a new aircraft fastened under the same ABC rotors. The twin GE engines would drive through a new main gearbox to a redesigned drive train and a shrouded tail propeller. There is little doubt that this could be the basis for an outstanding LHX contender.

Below: A camouflaged XH-59A with booster jets on flight test at the Army Aviation Development Test Activity at Fort Rucker. The ABC is now proven and ripe for taking to the next stage.

Sikorsky X-wing

Origin: Sikorsky Aircraft, USA.

Type: Stopped-rotor (high-speed VTOL) research aircraft, data S-72.

Engines: (Rotor drive and future rotor-blade blowing) two 1,500hp General Electric T58-5 turboshafts, (auxiliary propulsion) two 9,275lb (4207kg) thrust General Electric TF34-400A turbofans.

Dimensions: Diameter of (original) main rotor 62ft 0in (18·9m); span of wing 45ft 1·2in (13·75m); length (ignoring main rotor) 70ft 7in (21·52m); height overall 17ft 10·8in (5·46m); wing area 370sq ft (34·37m²).

Weights: Empty (compound configuration) 21,022lb (9535kg); max (compound) 26,200lb (11884kg).

Performance: Max speed (helicopter) 184mph (297km/h), (compound) 345mph (556km/h).

History: First flight 12 October 1976, (compound configuration) 10 April 1978, (as X-wing) programme begins late 1985.

User: USA (NASA/DARPA).

For 30 years designers have sought a method for combining the lift efficiency in the VTOL mode of a helicopter with the speed and efficiency in cruising flight of an aeroplane. One team that came close was Britian's National Gas Turbine Establishment where by using symmetric main-rotor blades, with air adherence enforced by high-energy blowing through full-span slits, it was found possible to stop the lifting rotor in mid air and proceed as an aeroplane, using the stopped blades for lift. In an alternative scheme the rotor could be folded away fore and aft in the top of the fuselage and a fixed wing used in cruising flight.

Later the idea was picked up by NASA Ames Research Center, which jointly with the US Army financed the construction of two special research aircraft, the Sikorsky S-72 RSRA (Rotor Systems Research Aircraft). This began flying as a conventional twin-turbine helicopter, but with amazing versatility to test new rotor ideas, including gimballed, articulated or hingeless rotors. It was the first helicopter to have ejection seats, the main rotor blades being severed in rapid sequence in the split second before firing of the seats (the system was successfully tested on the ground). The second RSRA was fitted with a variable-incidence fixed wing and twin turbofan propulsion engines. After

testing as a compound helicopter, using the wing and jet engines for high-speed cruise, the tail rotor was retained in further tests as a fixed-wing aircraft, including tailwheel taxi tests and flight to speeds up to the limit given above.

In January 1984 Sikorsky received a $76·9 million contract from NASA and DARPA to go the whole hog and, using an advanced circulation-controlled rotor with high-energy blowing from slits blasting downwards along both leading and trailing edges, slow down and stop the rotor in flight and convert to the full 345mph speed. The problem is that blades on one side of the aircraft have to reverse their airflow, the leading edge becoming the trailing edge (and the reverse happens on speeding up the rotor back into the helicopter mode). Moreover the two forward-facing blades behave like a forward-swept wing, needing immense strength and rigidity. The drive system, clutches and switchover of blowing from the original trailing edge to the new trailing edge also pose severe difficulties. The new composite rotor is bearingless and hingeless, flight control by quad digital fly-by-wire being effected by modulating the blowing through the various slits.

Above: Artist's impression of a future Sikorsky X-wing helicopter showing funding by DARPA (Defense Advanced Research Projects Agency) and the US Navy. Preliminary analyses showed that such a machine could have "approximately three times the range and speed capability of a conventional helicopter with equivalent payload lifting capability". In other words if may burn fuel at the same rate but, by going three times as fast, go three times as far. Such a prize is worth a lot of effort, and that is what it will take to get the X-wing flying.

Left: The RSRA (S-72) has been flying so far with a conventional S-61 engine/rotor system (and the landing gears of an F-5E). It is pictured after addition of the turbofans and wing.

OTHER SUPER-VALUE MILITARY GUIDES IN THIS SERIES......

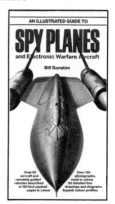

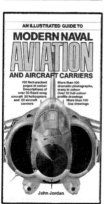

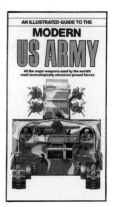

OTHER ILLUSTRATED MILITARY GUIDES NOW AVAILABLE.

Air War over Vietnam
Allied Fighters of World War II
Bombers of World War II
German, Italian and Japanese Fighters
   of World War II
Israeli Air Force
Military Helicopters
Modern Fighters and Attack Aircraft
Modern Soviet Air Force

Modern Soviet Navy
Modern Sub Hunters
Modern Submarines
Modern Tanks
Modern US Navy
Modern Warships
Pistols and Revolvers
Rifles and Sub-Machine Guns
World War II Tanks

* Each has 160 fact-filled pages
* Each is colourfully illustrated with hundreds of action photographs
  and technical drawings
* Each contains concisely presented data and accurate descriptions
  of major international weapons
* Each represents tremendous value

If you would like further information on any of our titles please write to:

Publicity Dept. (Military Div.), Salamander Books Ltd.,
27 Old Gloucester Street, London WC1N 3AF